Don't Turn Out the Lights

Don't Turn Out the Lights:

Entrepreneurship in Rural Saskatchewan

Al Scholz

University Extension Press
University of Saskatchewan
Saskatoon, Saskatchewan

Saskatchewan Council for
Community Development
Saskatoon, Saskatchewan

To order copies of this book, please contact:

U-Learn
Room 125, 117 Science Place
Saskatoon, Saskatchewan S7N 5C8

Phone: (306) 966•5565
Fax: (306) 966•5567
E-mail: u.learn@usask.ca

SCCD aims to be a catalyst for community co-operation, empowerment, and development in Saskatchewan.

P.O. Box 21038
Saskatoon, Saskatchewan S7H 5N9

Phone: (306) 975•6847
Fax: (306) 975•6850

Agriculture and Agri-Food Canada / Agriculture et Agroalimentaire Canada

Canada

Acknowledgement: Financial support for this book has been provided by the Canadian Adaptation and Rural Development in Saskatchewan (CARDS) Program. Funding for the CARDS Program is provided by Agriculture and Agri-Food Canada.

CANADIAN CATALOGUING IN PUBLICATION DATA

Scholz, Al, 1953 –

Don't turn out the lights: entrepreneurship in rural Saskatchewan

ISBN: 0 – 88880 – 418 – 0

1. Entrepreneurship—Saskatchewan—Case studies.
2. Rural development—Saskatchewan. 3. New business enterprises—Saskatchewan.
I. Title

HC117.S3 S39 2000 338'.04'097124 C00–920192–0

CREDITS:
Cover and Book Design: Jeremy Drought, Last Impression Publishing Service, Calgary, Alberta
Cartography: Marilyn Croot, Sun Mountain Graphics, Calgary, Alberta
Copy Editor: Donald Ward
Proofreader: Ursula Acton
Printed and bound in Canada by Houghton Boston, Saskatoon, Saskatchewan

Dedication

*To Lendy, my friend, wife, and business partner
who has developed her own entrepreneurial skills,
and our three wonderful and talented children
Aaron, Luke, and Elysse.*

Contents

Preface

THE idea for this book began in the mid-1990s when I was serving as Executive Director of the Saskatchewan Food Processors Association and later as Senior Consultant during the formation of the Apparel & Textile Association of Saskatchewan. After becoming familiar with both the food industry and the apparel and textile industry, I was surprised to realize one day that the majority of successful companies in these sectors are located throughout rural Saskatchewan. I kept meeting entrepreneurs and hearing their amazing success stories of innovation and creativity. In the face of the agriculture crisis and the predicted decline of rural communities, I knew these success stories needed to be told.

I began to write articles for newspapers and newsletters profiling some of the success stories in rural Saskatchewan. This led to a number of requests to be a guest speaker on rural enterprise development across Saskatchewan. These speaking engagements were well received and encouraged me to consider what more I could do to profile the many entrepreneurs across the province and to learn from their experience and success.

I thought a book that focused on optimism, recognized achievement, and celebrated success could play a small part in painting a different picture of rural Saskatchewan. As this idea was developing in my own mind, I discovered that a similar idea was taking shape within the Saskatchewan Council for Community Development (SCCD). They, too, had identified the need for a book on rural entrepreneurship, and they formed a committee to look at the idea of producing a book on rural success stories and Saskatchewan entrepreneurs. SCCD decided to proceed with the idea and applied for funds from the Canadian Adaptation and Rural Development in Saskatchewan (CARDS) Program to hire a writer and finance publication of the book. Together we collaborated on the vision and it was given to me to write the stories. My hope is this book will support new entrepreneurs and encourage our talented young people to stay in this province and start their own business.

Writing this book has been a fascinating experience. The best part has been the discussions I have enjoyed with entrepreneurs across the province. A special thanks goes to all those who were willing to be a part of this collection and make time in their busy lives to describe their experiences to me. I would also like to thank Linda Pipke and Sheila Ragush at SCCD for providing encouragement and administrative support for my research and writing, but more importantly, they shared the vision of the book and recognized the need for it.

Thank you also to the SCCD/CARDS committee that acted as an advisory group and helped select the businesses profiled in this book. They include Mich Ozeroff, Nick Postnikoff, Kevin Pulvermacher, Bruce Hobin, Bert Wolfe, Mark Richardson, and Linda Pipke. We made our final selection based on the different geographic regions in the province and a blend of different business sectors. The selection is far from exhaustive; countless other ventures could have been included.

I am a new writer and, like the entrepreneurs in the book, I have had to rely on the expertise of others. I am grateful to the University of Saskatchewan's Bert Wolfe, former Managing Editor of University Extension Press, and Bruce Hobin, Program Director, Agriculture, Food and Horticulture Programs—Extension Division. Both encouraged me in the early stages and committed themselves to publishing the book. Donald Ward was a great and patient editor. Perry Millar has guided the book through the press and been a great mentor.

Al Scholz
Saskatoon, Saskatchewan
August 2000

Centres of Entrepreneurial Success in Saskatchewan

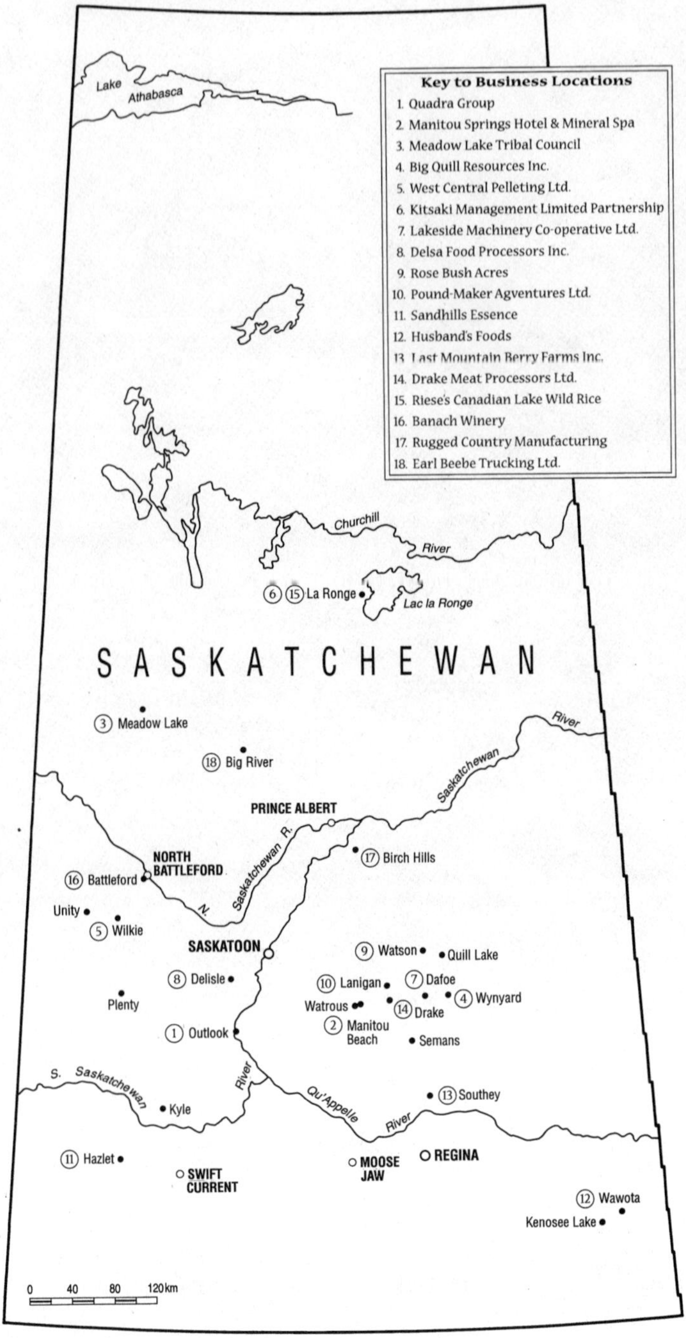

Introduction

WOULD THE LAST ONE TO LEAVE, PLEASE TURN OUT THE LIGHTS!" is a quip familiar to Saskatchewan residents, particularly in times of economic uncertainty. Yet the Human Development Index of the United Nations, which has consistently listed Canada as the best country in the world in which to live, lists Saskatchewan as the leading province in this great country. But do we celebrate this achievement? Not often enough! Modesty often does not allow us to admit that we are not only good, but the best!

"Saskatchewan," we are quick to tell ourselves—and anyone else who will listen—"is far from perfect." That may be true, but we're still better than anywhere else in the world.

By entitling this book *Don't Turn Out the Lights*, I want to turn the above saying on its head and suggest that it is not only tired but, as the stories in this book illustrate, no longer valid. This book was born out of the necessity to recognize and celebrate the people around us who have the passion, the vision, the energy, and the leadership to take a chance and do something new. In doing so they are contributing to the revitalization of the province, particularly its rural areas. The book is about personal initiative, creativity, community leadership, and achievement. It is about individuals and communities that have accomplished what many would have said was impossible. It is about entrepreneurs—Saskatchewan entrepreneurs. It may surprise us to learn that as entrepreneurs, we are among the best in the world. And we prove it every day! Our province is rich in both human and natural resources, and our products and services find their way into every corner of the globe.

This book was written particularly for young people, to support a vision of hope and an attitude of achievement. But it was also written for everyone else. Why? Because business success requires a team approach. While the entrepreneur is key, success also depends on committed managers, employees, and financial supporters who understand and believe in the vision.

Success resides in the people, not in any particular business. Business ventures, by their nature, can change and evolve monthly, even weekly, depending on local and world markets. A year from now some businesses may not be recognizable from the portraits painted in these pages; others may no longer even be operational. Successful entrepreneurs typically start many businesses throughout their careers. The point is, again, that the ultimate success of entrepreneurship resides in people's individual initiative, not a particular business.

There are many different types of business ventures that can have an impact on a community. Some might be individual efforts. Others might involve a group of entrepreneurs. Still others might be community enterprises. But all such ventures require a "driver" or a "project champion," someone with vision and passion who can provide leadership and the necessary focus for success. The entrepreneurs profiled in this book all share a deep and genuine passion for Saskatchewan and a powerful belief in the future of the province.

The world economy is in transition to a new model. How many of the entrepreneurial successes of today are based on the old model, and how many are anticipating new and emerging needs? The entrepreneurial successes of the past have largely been based on the precepts of an industrial, or production-driven economy. This model may not be suitable for the new economy, which is clearly market or demand driven. A clear message from all stories is "Know your customer."

Today, we hear that small business is driving the global economy. Many of the huge transnational corporations are divesting themselves of their subsidiaries in order to enjoy the creativity and greater possibilities for innovation to be found in smaller units. How much of this global business trend has rubbed off in Saskatchewan? Here, as elsewhere, barely thirty percent of new businesses survive the first year. Eighty-five percent don't last three years. Of those that survive the first five years, only fifty percent will make it to ten. These statistics have not changed during the past twenty years in Saskatchewan. Those who survive have learned to adapt to constantly changing market needs.

How have global trends affected Saskatchewan? A more important question might be, why do most of us have to struggle along the same dark path through the jungle of new business development? We're not sure where we're going, it's hot and sticky, we're short of supplies, and many of the team want to turn back. Are there not some lessons we can learn from one another? Do we all have to make the same mistakes? What are the fundamental factors of business success in Saskatchewan today? What do we mean by entrepreneurship? What is the definition of an entrepreneur?

These are some of the questions I asked myself when I first started working on this book. In my own career, I have worked with many successful entrepreneurs and business people. While most have taken a healthy, objective approach to government support programs and services, they have all relied largely on their own resources, initiative, and intuition. The common features of business success among Saskatchewan entrepreneurs include attitude, innovation, creativity, and tenacity. In addition, I have found that most entrepreneurs are willing to share their experiences of both success and failure in an effort to help new entrepreneurs. The objective of this book is to listen hard to those who have been successful. This is important, because there is great potential here and far too few entrepreneurs. We need to instill in our youth a vision of the entrepreneurial opportunities that are available to those with the vision to succeed.

Saskatchewan was opened to European settlement over a hundred years ago. But not everyone remained. The climate was harsh and the business environment difficult. Survival was made possible only through the development of new and creative ways of doing things. Those early settlers had a vision and a powerful belief that a prosperous economy and a rich society could be developed in this province. And they achieved their vision, as people took turns providing leadership for different ventures and initiatives. This is our history and our heritage.

This book is about entrepreneurship, but it is also about the rural leadership that continues to make a positive difference to the economic and social environment in this great province. As the eldest of five children born and raised on a 640-acre family farm near Churchbridge, I am a direct beneficiary of that leadership and courage. It is a difficult tradition to live up to, but I believe the twenty-first century belongs to Saskatchewan. We have the people, the resources, the institutions, and a history of personal initiative, innovation, and achievement. There is nothing holding us back.

I would like to conclude with a bit of rural philosophy we children often heard from our parents as encouragement to set our sights high and do our best:

It is better to aim for the sky and hit the post
than aim for the post and hit the ground.

Credit goes to my parents, Paul and Janet Scholz, for instilling a vision of achievement in all of us.

Community Ventures

1
Quadra Group

There is enormous business potential for agriculture and agribusiness in this province, and we happened to find it in the pork industry. We were looking for a business enterprise that had long-term growth and where Saskatchewan had distinct competitive natural advantages.

We have designed a process to successfully develop and manage state-of-the-art pork production operations in partnership with local communities. In total, we now employ over one hundred people in seventeen rural communities.

— Richard Wright, President of Quadra Group

THE three original partners—Richard Wright, Garth Larson, and Wayne Vermette—got their start in the pork industry as individual pig producers in the 1970s. They had always been interested in the larger industry issues, so it was natural that they would become involved in strategies for industry growth. The three got to know each other through the buying and selling of breeding stock and working together on the board of the provincial pork marketing agency in the early 1980s.

The 1980s was a time of adjustment and change in Canadian agriculture. The looming elimination of the Crow Rate had implications not only for grain exports, but was a clear signal for livestock producers as well. In addition to domestic changes, there were substantial shifts in global trading patterns as NAFTA and the new GATT agreements led to the World Trade Organization.

Richard, Garth, and Wayne knew that there was little chance as individual producers of capturing the benefits of an expanding global market for pigs. But how could they work together? A different approach was needed. After some initial research, they decided to develop their own model.

Management guru Tom Peters, co-author of *The Search for Excellence* and other books on management, talks of the need for innovators and entrepreneurs to take a "Ready, Fire, Aim" approach to business. No entrepreneur can know all the answers in advance. Certainly, you want to start with a clear vision of where you want to go, but there is no substitute for action. So "Ready, Fire" comes before "Aim—first you launch your idea, then you work hard to manage its direction.

The three partners adopted this approach when they decided to join forces as farmers and marketers in order to capitalize on emerging global trends. They put considerable planning into their vision—nothing less than a new concept for pork production. It was the need for a large and dependable supply of good-quality water that led them to locate the new business in Outlook in 1987.

"Along with the water came some funding support from the SIBED," Garth recalls, referring to the Saskatchewan Irrigation-Based Economic Development program, "but the area also had a good availability of quality feed grains."

It is common wisdom that farmers have an uncommon attachment to the land. Often it is a particular piece of land; sometimes it has been in the family for generations. This is where the Quadra partners first departed from the norm. They were all pig producers, but they lived in different parts of the province—Richard Wright in Wawota, Garth Larson in Semens, and Wayne Vermette in the Kyle district—and each of them willingly gave up his farm to relocate to the Outlook area.

In 1989 – 90, the partners raised $3 million to fund their initial project, Elite Stock Farm, a 600-hog operation established as a breeding stock multiplier unit for Pig Improvement (Canada) Ltd. (PIC). The Vermette family moved to the Elite site, eight kilometres south of Outlook (eighty kilometres south of Saskatoon), to supervise construction in 1989. Garth began working out of Outlook in the fall of 1990, and Richard relocated in 1993.

The second site was established in 1993, sixteen kilometres south east of town, to finish the barrows from the expansion of Elite that same year. This was the first operation the partners undertook that included broader participation from the community, and it was this operation that led to Quadra's community-based philosophy. The farm has since expanded to a 1,200-sow farrow-to-finish operation under the name of Great West Stock Farm (1996) Ltd.

Darren Swanson, who was responsible for the construction of the first barn, became the fourth partner, joining Quadra Group in 1995. The four partners are understandably pleased with their accomplishments, and justifiably proud. In twelve years, the operation has expanded to seventeen community-based pork operations with a current capacity of 500,000 pigs a year.

It is important to note the impact that succession planning had on the early business success of Quadra. They had a mechanism that allowed the original three partners to slowly phase into the Outlook operation full-time. It also allowed for partnership expansion to include Darren in 1995 and for Wayne Vermette to leave the partnership in 1998. "We knew from previous business experience that you must have a succession plan and be prepared for constant change," says Richard. "Allowances must be made in any business organization for partners to come in and for others to leave."

In many ways, Richard Wright is a most unlikely pig farmer. The son of a clergyman who served rural parishes across western Canada and Ontario, Richard spent his formative years in Saskatchewan, but went on to graduate with a degree in chemical engineering from the Royal Military College of Canada in 1965. He served in the Royal Canadian Navy for seven years, after which he worked in market development for Canadian Pacific Ltd. His career with CP took him to Montreal, Winnipeg, and Edmonton, where he gained valuable experience in managing both people and projects. But deep inside, he felt, there was something missing.

"I don't know if I wanted more of a challenge," he reflects, "but I did have a tremendous urge to go where the real work was done. I literally felt that I wanted to get my hands dirty. I had the intuitive feeling that getting into some kind of farm enterprise was the right thing for me, but we also had to make money at it."

On leaving CP Rail, Richard and his wife, Dianne, looked across the prairies for several months before settling on the Wawota farm in 1975. As an existing pig production facility, it suited their initial needs. But Richard decided that, if he was going to be in pigs, he might as well be in the elite breeding section of the industry, and he was soon operating as an independent breeding stock multiplier for PIC, the world's leading genetic and breeding company.

Not surprisingly, Richard's involvement in the industry went far beyond the barn. He served for eleven years as a director with the SPI Marketing Group, and he was chair of the board from 1989 to 1993. Again not surprisingly, his vision for the Saskatchewan hog industry has grown with his relationship with PIC. The first Quadra hog operation in Outlook was also an elite breeder farm on contract to PIC. PIC has long recognized the natural advantages of a Saskatchewan location for one of its four nucleus breeding herds in the world. With its sparse population, the province provides producers with the ability to isolate each farm for disease control, and there is low risk of infection from neighbouring farms.

"The location of the PIC breeder farm in this province adds yet another tremendous natural competitive advantage to Saskatchewan pork producers," Richard says. "In addition, the University of Saskatchewan has the Western College for Veterinary Medicine, with a swine specialty, plus the Veterinary Infectious Disease Organization (VIDO), the Prairie Swine Centre, Inc., and the Prairie Feed Resource Centre, which are large research initiatives aimed at further increasing the competitive advantage for pig and other livestock producers."

Quadra Group has been a key player in creating a critical mass of large, community-owned pig producers in this province. According to Richard, "We now have many of the elements to make Saskatchewan, and the other prairie provinces, one of the world's leading producers of high quality pork products for the world. Now all we need is steady and prudent expansion in the number of producers and barns across the province. We need literally millions of Saskatchewan-produced pigs each year in order to support the complete development of the pork value-chain from the farm to the consumer."

Clearly, the real benefit of an integrated agricultural industry is the creation of wealth and employment in the transportation, processing, storage, marketing, and distribution systems as Saskatchewan pork products make their way to retailers around the world. Wright is passionate about this vision: "We must try to do as much in Saskatchewan, or within the prairie region, as we can. Why give up the large profit margins to processors outside the prairie region or outside the country?"

Quadra Group has always had the big picture in mind. They encouraged the location of the elite breeder nucleus farm in Saskatchewan, and they have consistently supported the University's research activities. Now they are working with other production units to integrate into the value-chain to the consumer, "so we can continue to capture maximum returns for our farmer members," says Wright.

Bob Hamilton, president of the Eagle Creek Stock Farm in Plenty, Saskatchewan, describes the success of Quadra Group in terms of the community: "Our community was one of the first Quadra expansion units. We were looking for a viable agribusiness enterprise with the size and scale that permitted state-of-the-art technology and management systems. We found what we were looking for with Quadra Group. A number of small rural communities were brought

Eagle Creek Pork Producers Ltd., the first Quadra expansion unit, 1,200-sow farrow-to-finish operation near Plenty, SK

together for this project. Our view of communities must become larger and have a regional focus. We have to start working together and reduce the competitiveness between individual rural communities."

Plenty and the neighbouring towns of Stranraer, Ruthhilda, Dodsland, Kelfield, Handel, and Herschel, are all feeling the positive effects of the 1,200-sow farrow-to-finish operation. With nine full-time and several part-time employees, Eagle Creek Stock Farm has given a tremendous economic boost to the whole area. Spin-offs include support for the local infrastructure: roads, schools, and local businesses.

It was working with Bob Odermatt and his Beechy group, and Bob Hamilton and his group, that helped Quadra come up with a unique system for raising investment capital. Early on in their development, Quadra had wanted to expand, but with a minimum of two years from initiation to commissioning the facility, and another two years before the enterprise becomes profitable, it was impossible to find commercial investors who were willing to put up the necessary $3.6 million, given that the concept was new and the expansion unproven.

Once again, they had to think of an alternative. With professional help, they developed a community investment system that has since been replicated sixteen times in Saskatchewan and Manitoba, with more in the planning stages. Briefly, the system provides farmers with a mechanism for direct investment, ownership, and control of pig production in the enterprise. They receive some tax benefits from the arrangement, plus the right to supply the operation with feed grains and utilize the by-products as organic fertilizer.

"There is money in rural Saskatchewan, but investors are cautious," said Richard. "If the business idea is sound, adequate capital can be secured. We are only one example of several successful community-based agribusiness enterprises. There are a number of other creative enterprises across Saskatchewan that are paving the road to the future."

"We've broken new ground," Bob Hamilton concurs. "We've been able to create jobs, growth, and expansion in our home area. Quadra not only provides us with the design and management, but they continue to be on the leading edge of productivity innovation. One of the Quadra barns has recently been recognized as one of the top thirteen most efficient hog barns in North America, with a per-sow weaning rate of 25.4 per year. This is only possible through management and staffing excellence at every aspect of the operation, Quadra's training systems, and their belief that Saskatchewan people are world-class."

Richard Wright learned a few things about himself while he was working with the military and with CP Rail: "I found that I had a knack for quietly and earnestly working with people, and for organizing a team approach to management and innovation. As individuals, we all have a few key strengths. But no one of us has enough to do it on our own."

The Quadra partners have complementary skills, and they have acquired staff to fill the gaps. In addition, according to Garth, "We learned to make the best use of professionals early in the process, so that the business side of the business is done right the first time. It is only with empowered teams that we can attain excellence in all areas of the administration, production, management, and marketing systems."

There are enormous advantages to the Quadra model. Doing everything at one location helps to reduce stress and maximize disease control and weight gain in the farrow-to-finish process. In addition, every barn has a feed processing plant, so local producers benefit from supplying the 8,000 tonnes per year of wheat, barley, peas, and other feed grains required by each 1,200-sow barn. This takes a lot of acres into a local market.

At the global level, the Quadra system now has the capability of providing one million pigs to a processor and retailer, and each of those animals will be of the same consistent high quality. Each comes from the same breeding stock. Each has been given the same feed, the same management, the same quality control system. This provides enormous benefits to investors, and it gives the Quadra Group leverage in developing strong links up the value-chain.

Taking another big step toward fulfilling the founders' vision, Quadra Group has recently entered into a strategic alliance with Fletcher's Fine Foods, Ltd. The arrangement gives Fletcher's exclusivity over pigs produced by the seventeen independent operations in the Quadra family. Quadra Group and Fletcher's have also entered into formal discussions regarding the possible exchange of minority ownership interests.

"This transaction sets the stage for a new era for both Quadra and Fletcher's," says Richard Wright. "By aligning our interests and implementing a long-term contractual arrangement, which includes downside pricing protection for both parties, we improve each other's risk and long-term profitability profile."

"We have come a long way toward achieving our vision of developing a pig production chain from the farmer to the consumer," says Garth Larson. "In the process, we have also built sustainable and sound business enterprises in rural communities that generate jobs for our youth and create wealth for the province."

"In our opinion," Richard concludes, "there is a tremendous future for prairie farmers and rural communities if we work together, continue to be innovative, and look at what the market demands. If we are successful, we can play a key role in the changing food system in a way that meets our needs as a family of rural communities."

2

Manitou Springs Hotel & Mineral Spa

There is passion, energy, enthusiasm, and vision in most communities. It takes some basic organizational structure to pull key leaders together to make it happen. We constantly fed on each other's energy, which helped, because we all had turns of frustration. There was always someone who was enthusiastic and kept us going. As a committee, we took bold action and took risks, such as proceeding with the planning and construction of the spa before we had all the money. This created a lot of controversy at the time, but in my opinion, if we had not acted boldly it would have never happened.

— Murray Westby, member of the committee

THE reclamation of Manitou Beach as a resort community was an economic miracle. When fire destroyed the Chalet mineral water pool, the community's last tourist attraction, the local economy appeared doomed. But the fire turned out to be the spark for a new initiative to rebuild not only the pool, but the community as well.

A small group of community and business leaders who shared a vision for a new approach to business redeveloped the resort. It is thanks to these individuals that today there is a prosperous spa, hotels, several motels and bed-and-breakfast establishments, a renovated and re-energized Danceland hall, one of the best golf courses in the province, and a fully serviced RV Park and campground, not to mention a new mandate for Camp Easter Seal and a booming resort and conference-centre business that has created combined employment for over a hundred people—many of them young people who have found management and marketing jobs in the hospitality and service industries.

"I grew up in the 1950s with all the glamour of a prosperous and vigorous vacation location," Lionel Sproule recalls. His parents owned the Chalet swimming pool. "My wife and I hung on to the swimming pool for a number of years, together with friends, but we sold it a few years before the place burned down in 1983."

Lionel was not involved in the early stages of the planning for the new facility: "We were living in Regina, and thought we had severed the links with our past. However, a group of local people started to do something to re-build the community. Their enthusiasm for a new vision drew us back to Manitou Beach, and we became intensely involved."

Manitou Beach was in its heyday in the 1940s and early 1950s, when it was the premier vacation and holiday location for many people across western Canada. Its facilities included swimming pools, hotels, and a dance hall that featured leading big bands from across Canada and the United States. Some came simply for recreation, some for vigorous entertainment, and some for therapy as they took advantage of the natural salts in the lake.

The Manitou Beach resort began its slow slide into decline in the 1960s. With improved highways, travel trailers, and economy air travel, prairie people were increasingly leaving the province for their vacations and recreational activities. The west coast, the Rocky Mountains, Hawaii, and various locations in the United States became the premier holiday destinations, and by the 1970s Manitou Beach had become a shadow of its former self.

By the early 1980s, however, the resort had failed. The beach had been operating in the same manner since the 1930s. The supporting businesses had closed. The tourist trade had essentially collapsed. The Chalet swimming pool remained open, but it was very old, and the fire that destroyed it sounded the death knell for Manitou Beach. It was the last straw. The collapse of the community appeared imminent.

The immediate challenge facing the group of community and business leaders was money. Their ideas and vision would require literally millions of dollars. But, with true Saskatchewan optimism, they set aside the nagging issue of "how" they would finance their large venture to concentrate on "what" they needed to do.

First, they decided to build a year-round health spa rather than simply rebuild the swimming pool. It was a leap of faith. At the time, the idea of a year-round mineral spa in Saskatchewan was unheard of. In addition, for fifty years various officials had been challenging the community's claims about the health benefits that could be derived from the mineral waters. In the early 1950s the resort had lost its status as a provincial park, along with the attendant government revenues, partly because the government of the time had rejected the health and therapy claims made by Manitou Beach supporters and business people.

Almost in defiance, the planning group decided to focus their market development on the mineral spa. They knew the health aspect was a growing market, and recreation was still a feature that would draw people to the resort.

"There was some very clear thinking at this stage," says Dale Hayter, the current owner of the hotel and spa, "that was the result of having experienced professional and business people in the group. We had the benefit of their understanding of the consumer market and a business sense of what would work."

They also had dedication and determination. The committee met every Sunday morning for over four years. They held over 200 meetings. This constant involvement was essential to the success of the venture. It served to maintain the enthusiasm at a high level, and it greatly facilitated communication and the co-ordination of activities. Without the long-term commitment of these twenty or twenty-five people, the venture would have never happened. There were lots of reasons to quit, but the entrepreneurial features of focus, persistence, and perseverance kept them going.

The committee got to the stage of believing that a new hotel would be necessary to accommodate the people who wanted to take advantage of the spa. Builders estimated a combined hotel and spa would cost from $6 to $8 million. They decided to begin with the spa, and purchased the same lots on which the original swimming pool had stood.

They made the decision to go ahead in 1986 – 87, but no one knew for sure how it would be financed. In many ways, it was the worst of times to begin raising capital. The province had had a dry year and a poor crop, and the economy as a whole was heading downhill.

The group tried to sell the project as an investment, but it was a hard sell. "We used the history of Manitou Beach as a marketing tool for investors," says Sproule. "We approached people who had been part of the resort as a child or young adult and tugged at the memories and the great times."

They decided to commence the fund raising and the design work at the same time. The group considered it an essential move if they were to convince potential investors that something was actually going to happen. So they started spending

Manitou Springs Hotel & Mineral Spa at Manitou Beach, near Watrous, SK. Located in the centre of Saskatchewan's potash belt, it has a world-famous reputation for its healing properties.

money before they had any. In retrospect, according to Sproule, "This turned out to be the best decision. It created a sense of optimism, but it was done at great personal risk. It was the right thing to do, otherwise we would have never got started."

The group started the design work with a firm in Edmonton that specialized in swimming pools, but they soon parted ways. The Edmonton firm could not agree on construction standards and parameters. The Manitou Beach Committee knew from experience that the mineral water would eat up normal concrete and any metal components that were installed under water. Brine shrimp also had to be screened out. It became apparent that local information would be critical to the construction of the facility, and in the end the committee became their own contractors.

No one on the committee had any experience at raising money, but once again they plunged in. Five or six people in the planning group agreed to invest $25,000 each in order to get the fund-raising started. Later, other members of the committee invested $10,000 to $15,000 each. Seed money, they believed, was required to attract community money.

But this was to be a business venture. They would accept only investments, no donations. Again, it was a hard sell. Many elderly people who attended Town Hall meetings in the surrounding communities were not interested in investing in a business. Many people said that the government should build the spa and hotel, because it was a resort and the government would benefit. The group acknowledged that government could have a role, but they were adamant that this would be primarily a business venture.

They sold shares at $1,000 each. People could buy a single share or blocks of shares, individually or as a group. Unfortunately, they stalled at $18,000, and the group hired a firm to fund-raise on commission.

"That was a disaster," says Sproule. "They simply went back to the same local people we had approached and caused confusion. We terminated them after a couple of months and decided we must do it alone, but be more business-like about it." Arnold Strueby, mayor of Manitou Beach, took on the task of co-ordinating their efforts and sold the majority of the shares.

The timing was right for the government to take a role. The committee had learned a great deal about what did and what did not work, and they had reorganized their marketing approach to focus on the remembrance and history of the resort. The government of the day had recently introduced a venture capital program, with a thirty percent tax credit for investors. A meeting with Premier Grant Devine resulted in a commitment of $430,000 from the government if the community could raise $500,000.

The committee formed the "New Era Venture Capital Corporation," made new applications, and started an aggressive selling campaign. The government program turned out to be critical, as many potential investors who had felt they could not support the venture unless it had some assurance of government backing started coming on board.

"People will do anything to avoid paying taxes," Murray Westby philosophizes, "and the thirty percent tax credit made all the difference."

The thirty percent tax credit was only good for Saskatchewan residents. This turned out to be a hindrance as the committee took their investment package beyond the local community and across the province, for they found many people outside Saskatchewan who were interested and willing to invest. And the approach was costly in terms of both cash and time. Individual members of the planning committee continued to slip their own money into the pot to show steady growth, and they issued regular press releases to generate and maintain enthusiasm.

They had a deadline for raising the $500,000. They asked for one extension, and got it. Soon afterward, holding out the carrot of $430,000 in government funds, they achieved their goal of $500,000. Overnight the fund went to $930,000 as the government added in its $430,000 to the pot. In the end they had $1.3 million, which was still short of the $2 million that would be necessary to build.

Once again, amid considerable criticism this time, the committee decided to "just do it." They looked for creative ways to reduce costs. They took advantage of the "New Careers Project" that provided opportunities for people on Employment Insurance and welfare to be re-trained for a new career. This helped keep the project community oriented, and provided opportunities for local people to be directly involved in the construction.

The spa commenced business early in 1988, with the official opening in June of that year. The New Era Venture Capital Corporation had worked well. The $2.5 million spa opened with a debt of some $800,000, but a good deal of equity. The success of the launch of the spa encouraged the committee to commence Phase II, the construction of the hotel.

It is important to note that the finance and building sub-committee carried on as the management committee. Lionel Sproule became the business and operations manager, and managed the facility for the first four years. This was critical for the success of the next stage, which was building the hotel. The same commitment and determination was required to make the hotel work as well as the spa. The continuing involvement of the same people was the key to the success of the whole project.

A separate Venture Capital Corporation was established for the hotel. The committee remained the same, but a number of new investors came forward. This proved helpful. There were about 300 shareholders in each corporation and about 150 common shares.

The total cost for the hotel was $4 million. A federal/provincial grant of $800,000 provided an incentive for investors to raise the required $550,000 to trigger the payment of the grant. The hotel opened in 1991.

The committee owned and operated the hotel and spa until March 1998. While it had taken hard work and a gargantuan leap of faith to get it started, they found it was hard work to keep the hotel and spa going. It was fun to a point, but with sixty to seventy people on the payroll, and a business that was highly competitive, people soon grew tired. Many had risked their life savings, others their businesses, to make it happen. Their intent had been to rebuild the community, not to own and manage it. It was time to pass the responsibility to someone else who could focus on the effective marketing and management of the business.

The decision to sell took time, but eventually Dale Hayter, one of the original investors, made an offer to the shareholders. It was accepted. The hotel and spa are now effectively and efficiently in private hands. Shareholders in the hotel received 92% of their share value, plus the tax concessions that they had received in the beginning. The spa shareholders received 100% of their share value, in addition to a dividend they had received on their investment in the first year of operation. In brief, the shareholders were all able to get their investment back, and some with interest.

The Manitou Springs Hotel & Mineral Spa is currently in an expansion phase based on its continuing growth. An outside deck tavern has been enclosed, and VLT machines are available. Two eight-person hot tubs have been added for hotel guests. Most important is a new facility for hyperbaric oxygen therapy (HBOT), a medical treatment that uses pure oxygen to alleviate hypoxia, or the lack of oxygen, in cells. The HBOT chamber takes spa therapy to another level. Guests come from across western Canada for the spa, and Dale Hayter is adding twelve new modular rooms with light housekeeping suites to accommodate those who come for extended treatment.

Manitou Beach continues to be a popular conference centre owing to its central location in the province and a range of activities outside the spa. Dale will expand the hotel to 100 rooms in 2000 to accommodate the growing demand.

"The door is now open for whatever we want to do," he says. "We are proof that very small communities can do anything they want if there is a clear vision for the future and a commitment to fulfil the dream. The next step is to market our facilities and community as a destination location to the United States. With the advantages of the Canadian dollar, plus our therapy and recreation facilities, we expect huge success in the future."

3

Meadow Lake Tribal Council

Employee buyouts of failing companies rarely succeed. In this case, the employees of a failing sawmill company teamed up with local First Nations bands to create a successful corporate turnaround.

ON April 24, 1998, the Meadow Lake Tribal Council became 100 percent owners of NorSask Forest Products Inc., one of the province's largest companies. The deal, which was years in the making, was an opportunity for the shareholders to realize the true value of spirit, dedication, and sheer tenacity—of sweat equity, in other words. In 1999, NorSask and its sister companies generated approximately $51 million in local economic activity through employment alone.

A new approach to economic development is emerging among the First Nations in Canada. This approach emphasizes the creation of profitable businesses to compete in the global economy. These business ventures are expected to help First Nations achieve their broader objectives of self-determination, greater control over activities on their traditional lands, and economic self-sufficiency.

Key elements of this emerging development strategy are education, institution building, and the acquisition of land and resources, as well as the formation of business alliances among aboriginal and non-aboriginal companies. At the same time, there are a growing number of non-aboriginal corporations and companies who are proactively adopting business alliances with First Nations people as part of their strategy for long-term corporate survival.

The economic development activity among key non-aboriginal investors and nine First Nations of the Meadow Lake Tribal Council is an excellent example of this new approach to community economic development in action.

"Looking back over ten years, the NorSask venture has been an incredible journey," says Vern Bachiu, Director of Policy and Development for the Meadow Lake Tribal Council. "The business was started under the worst possible conditions, but the vision of a small group of leaders and entrepreneurs made it what it is today."

The Meadow Lake Sawmill was built in 1971 by investors from the United States to complement a proposed pulp mill. It was managed initially by a group from the States, and typically employed eighty to a hundred people. The community hoped that the sawmill and proposed pulp mill would provide a large number of good jobs for many years. Unfortunately, the pulp mill was never built, and less than six years later the management team returned to the United States, leaving Prince Albert Pulpwood to manage the sawmill. Operations declined for ten years, then it was sold to the provincial government in 1986 and operated under the Crown Management Board as NorSask Forest Products.

The working conditions were awful, according to Allen Brander, who was general manager of the sawmill for two years. "The biggest problem was that the mill was designed for U.S. weather, not the freezing temperatures we have here for most of the winter." Despite its design flaws, though, Brander believed the mill could make money if it was done right.

In 1988 the mill, which had been losing $1 – 2 million a year, was put up for sale. The provincial government of the day was in the business of privatizing community ventures, and mechanisms for employee-ownership transfers had been developed. But, as Brander says, "it was very hard to convince people that we could make this work. A deal like the NorSask deal just never happens by itself."

In the end, a few people took enormous risks and charged ahead.

About eighty employees of the sawmill got together and formed a company called Techfor Services. They bought fifty percent of NorSask from the Crown Investment Corporation (CIC), and invited The Meadow Lake Tribal Council to purchase another fifty percent and be an equal partner. The Tribal Council was a purely political body at the time, and the move to business development was a dramatically new initiative, requiring its own negotiations with the nine First Nations in the region. It was Chief Percy Derocher's vision that his people become not merely stakeholders in forest activities, but shareholders with responsibility and a voice at the boardroom table.

With almost twenty years experience as sawmillers, the employees had definite ideas about how to improve the mill so it could operate year round and provide

Aerial view of NorSask Forest Products Inc., Meadow Lake, SK. Photo: Concept 3.

stable employment. With professional accounting and legal advice, a deal was struck between Techfor Services and the Meadow Lake Tribal Council to buy 100% of the shares in NorSask Forest Products from the Saskatchewan Crown Investment Corporation, with the CIC retaining an option to purchase twenty percent of NorSask Products.

Two things were critical to NorSask's operations: access to a reliable source of timber, and a plan for managing the forest so it would stay healthy and productive. Concurrent with the formation of the new company, NorSask signed a Forest Management License Agreement with the province. The agreement gave NorSask the right to harvest over a 3.3 million-hectare land base. With an annual harvest of about 5,000 hectares, of which 30% is softwood, NorSask could proceed with its business plan, knowing the mill's appetite for fibre could be satisfied without jeopardizing its forest resource.

In the summer of 1991, Millar Western Pulp, a family-owned forest product company from Whitecourt, Alberta, was invited by the province to construct and operate the world's first zero-effluent, 100% aspen pulp mill. CIC exercised its option to sell/transfer twenty percent of NorSask Forest Products to the Meadow Lake Pulp Partnership, a company owned 50-50 by CIC and Millar Western Pulp.

The consortium of NorSask, the Meadow Lake Pulp Partnership, and Mistik (a newly formed joint venture) had successfully—and literally—created a forest industry in north-west Saskatchewan.

In 1991 Mistik Management Ltd., which is owned 50-50 by NorSask Forest Products and the Meadow Lake Pulp Partnership, was created to oversee the Forest Management License Agreement. Mistik carried the responsibility of managing the forest in a sustainable manner, supplying product to the sawmill and pulp mill, monitoring regrowth, and contracting suppliers to build roads and plant seedlings. Mistik was the first company in Canada to complete a full environment impact assessment for a logging plan, and it won an ABEX (Achievement in Business Excellence) Award as a result. Environmental sensitivity was seen as crucial to the practice of historical aboriginal values relating to stewardship of the land and caring for creation.

How did this happen in a few short years? According to Vern Bachiu, it was possible "because of a very small group of leaders and entrepreneurs who had a vision for the future. Certainly Allen Brander, the NorSask General Manager and CEO of the new company, was the driver of the vision."

Chief Percy Derocher, Chief of the Meadow Lake Tribal Council, was the other partner in the entrepreneurial mix. He understood the vision Allen Brander was presenting to aboriginal and non-aboriginal people alike. Together, they provided the spark and enthusiasm, not to mention the trust and the credibility, to move forward. Chief Derocher knew that First Nations people needed to get involved in economic ventures to balance their emerging opportunities in social and political self-sufficiency. It had never been done before, but Chief Percy moved forward with a creative, common-sense approach to include economic development among the Tribal Council's interests and responsibilities. They had little to lose and everything to gain by joining forces with Allen Brander.

The third driving force was Ray Ahenakew, CEO of the Tribal Council. Ray Ahenakew was born in Sandy Lake near Shellbrook, but grew up in Saskatoon. He did not attend high school, but his life experience has been at least the equivalent of a PhD. He is a charismatic man with enormous energy. Playing semi-professional hockey for a number of years sharpened his leadership skills. Never satisfied with half-measures, when he became involved in First Nations politics he rose to the level of Vice-Chief of the Federation of Saskatchewan Indian Nations. Subsequent to that, he served for three years as President of the Saskatchewan Indian Institute for Technologies, a post-secondary training institution. For the past fifteen years, he has been CEO of the Meadow Lake Tribal Council, and has been instrumental in setting a course for change that will secure a future for all people in the community. It was Ray's energy and influence that provided much of the cement in the early years that bound the partnerships of NorSask together.

The enterprise was joint-ventured with the chiefs who were willing to work with Allen Brander and Techfor Services. Techfor Services, consisting of union and non-union, aboriginal and non-aboriginal owners, is complicated enough. Throw in a plant that hasn't been profitable since it was built, and you should have the makings of a financial disaster.

"It was not your typical recipe for success," Bachiu recalls. But he has an explanation: "Allen Brander made a large, personal business investment and became one of the major shareholders. He had the most at risk. His vision and enthusiasm attracted the rest of the investor partners."

Allen Brander grew up in the Meadow Lake region. His father was in the sawmill business, and Allen had a natural inclination for it. According to Bachui, "Allen has the mind of an engineer combined with the business sense of an MBA graduate."

The business was on the verge of collapse several times during the first three years, owing largely to an aggressive modernization program and a dramatically changed cost structure. Computerization was introduced to boost quality and production, and the workforce was reduced from 125 to eighty-five. The mill's unionized workers supported the move, which took courage and foresight, considering Techfor Services was largely owned by unionized employees.

Another key to NorSask's success was a clear marketing strategy: the company would sell on margin rather than on a cash basis. Early in 1990, this policy put the company under severe pressure from employees, partners, and the banks, as the company was cash short and could not make its payroll. The yards were loaded with inventory, but management resisted selling. They desperately needed the cash but, as Allen Brander explains, if they had sold at that time, "we would have sustained losses that would never be recovered. We held firm to our business and marketing policy, and worked incredibly hard to obtain additional bank financing for the payroll. Within weeks lumber prices jumped, we sold at good margins, and the rest is history."

Brander's strategy underlines the importance of a thorough understanding of the industry you are working in, and having a partner you trust who can make those difficult calls. "Maybe it is partly luck," Bachiu reflects, "but it is also partly an assertive approach to business development with all stakeholders. It requires excellent communication, trust, and mutual respect."

The Meadow Lake Tribal Council takes in nine individual First Nations, including the Cree First Nations: Canoe Lake, Flying Dust, Island Lake, Makwa Sahgaiehcan, Waterhen Lake, and the Dene First Nations: Birch Narrows, Buffalo River, Clearwater River, and English River. The non-aboriginal communities in this region include Meadow Lake, Gregg Lake, Makwa, Loon Lake, Goodsoil, and Pierceland to the south, and the more northerly communities of Green Lake, Cole Bay, Jans Bay, Beauval, Pinehouse, Ile à la Crosse, Patuanak, Buffalo Narrows, St. George's Hill, Michel Village, La Loche, and Turnor Lake. According to census estimates, there are approximately 8,000 aboriginal and 16,600 non-aboriginal people in this region. Of the latter, approximately 5,000 are Métis.

The Meadow Lake Tribal Council had always enjoyed a good working relationship with these communities, aboriginal and the non-aboriginal alike. The skills of Ray Ahenakew were no small part of that success. Similarly, there was "good chemistry" between Allen Brander and Chief Percy Derocher, and they each had enormous credibility in both communities.

"Any community-based economic development must draw on local leaders that have proven themselves in the business world," says Vern Bachiu. "There is less resistance to trying something new if the community knows that the leadership is made up of people who are proven leaders and already successful in business."

However, as Vern describes, at times the leadership switched back and forth: "Sometimes Allen provided the 'good leadership' and the Tribal Council provided 'good followship,' but this changed back and forth depending on the nature of the developments. It has been a great partnership."

On April 24, 1998 a deal was struck among the shareholders, and the Meadow Lake Tribal Council became the sole owner of NorSask, buying all shares in Techfor Services and Millar Western Pulp. The acquisition allowed the original investors to liquidate their equity and made the Tribal Council the largest aboriginal-owned forest products company in Canada. Soon the Meadow Lake Tribal Council was working to help other aboriginal communities in Canada and internationally to develop models for economic self-sufficiently.

Ray Ahenakew, a key player in this aspect of the business, has spent the past four years developing a new role for NorSask. During the revolution in Nicaragua in the early 1990s a number of aboriginal peoples from the Miskito First Nations moved to Canada as refugees. Coming from huge timber reserves in Nicaragua, they asked the Government of Canada if there were any First Nations with expertise in forest management. Industry Canada approached the Meadow Lake Tribal Council, whose help and support has led to a number of trips and feasibility studies in Nicaragua.

As a result, a joint venture company, Makwa International, has been formed between the Meadow Lake Tribal Council and the Nicaragua Miskito Indians, with the Tribal Council holding a fifty-one percent controlling share. The investment to date has been mostly time, as most of the cash costs have been offset by development funding. There are development loans available from the World Bank and the Inter-American Development Bank for this type of economic venture.

Many aboriginal communities have the same characteristics that are associated with small rural communities throughout the prairie region in terms of population, demographics, size, location, and reliance on the land base. Acknowledging this, some First Nations have realized that, to succeed in the global economy, they must form business alliances with other people and groups in their region.

The Meadow Lake Tribal Council experience is a model for the countless other small communities that dot the prairie landscape and face the same challenges of isolation and depleting populations. The strength of this community-based approach is its ability to create viable business ventures while at the same time maintaining the traditional cultural values that are important to the community.

What is the recipe for success in such a collection of communities? The key ingredients were vision, leadership, trust, mutual respect, and a willingness to work extremely hard for the benefit of all.

4

Big Quill Resources Inc.

I am convinced that every community has the financial and human resources available locally to do anything. Building a good team is the most important part of the formula for success. Yes, we need leaders and visionaries but we also need a group of committed people who can focus on the day-to-day details and get the job done.

We proved it in Wynyard. We have built a multi-million dollar, globally competitive mineral processing company with exports throughout North America. We did it with local people and local investments. Since start-up in 1991, we have doubled production capacity every two years.

— Harvey Haugen, President of Big Quill Resources Inc.

BIG QUILL is a good example of a community-based enterprise that focused on utilizing community resources, both human and financial, to produce an industrial product for national and international markets.

"The story of Big Quill Resources Inc. can be told in two ways," says President Harvey Haugen. "The first is to understand *what* we were able to do as a small community group with limited financial resources. The other part of the story is *how* we did it. The *how* is really the key. It was done through recognizing the huge human resource potential that I believe is available in most communities. In our case, it was driven and sustained by a 'can-do' attitude that led to creative problem-solving and innovation."

To start with the *what*, though, the Big Quill processing plant came into existence in 1983 when the Potash Corporation of Saskatchewan (PCS) began looking for new products and markets. They were investigating an ion exchange method of producing potassium sulphate by using the saltwater body at Big Quill

Lake. Sodium sulphate (salt water) is extracted from the lake and combined with potassium chloride (potash) in an ion exchange process that creates potassium sulphate, one of the ingredients used in making wallboard.

PCS did their initial research in Florida. Once it was determined to be feasible, a pilot plant was constructed on the edge of Big Quill Lake near Wynyard. From 1986 to 1990, Harvey Haugen led a group of PCS technicians who were working to find a way to make the process commercially viable. They had just developed what Harvey refers to as "a creative, homegrown innovation" to the Florida-based technology that allowed them to increase their output and become commercially viable when word came that PCS had decided to pull the plug on the pilot venture.

It was in the fall of 1990 that PCS gave its Big Quill employees notice that the plant would be shut down. "Looking back on it," Harvey reflects, "you can see why they did it. PCS had purchased some very large companies. Our pilot plant was very small, highly developmental, and I don't think it really fit into what they were doing or where they were going at that time. However, our group had worked hard at developing the process, and we were absolutely convinced it would work. So we got a small group of employees together and decided to buy the pilot plant from PCS." To the corporation's credit, PCS allowed them to keep the plant operating for almost another year while the purchase deal was being completed in the fall of 1991.

The first thing they did was take a trip to Saskatoon to talk with Great Western Brewery, a highly successful company that had recently been bought from the parent company by its local employees. Peter McCann, the president at the time, emphasized the importance of making sure the employee investors all put money on the table. They had to make a decision, he said, and they had to make it with money.

Initially, six people put down $100 each, with the understanding that they would never see it again. "It was the first investment," Haugen recalls, "and it was very significant, because we were not very sophisticated and at the time there was not a lot of cash around. The $100 down meant that we were in."

Of course, it was a major challenge to finance a take-over by a small group of employees. The next step was a community bond offering that successfully raised the $800,000 needed to purchase the plant. It cost the group $50,000 in legal fees and expenses to raise the money and finalize the deal. And there were long stretches of anxious waiting before the final turnover of the keys.

Big Quill Resources Inc., a potassium sulphate processing plant, at Big Quill Lake, SK.

When the new owners took over on September 1, 1991, they were confident enough to shut the plant down and begin construction on the addition that would house their new ion exchange process. They knew they had to increase production from 2,500 tonnes per year to at least 7,000 tonnes per year based on the new process. The addition would allow them to install a new system that would bring them up to commercial scale, with enough volume to supply industrial markets.

The new system was installed, plus a granulation system that would allow the company to produce granular fertilizer for the agriculture industry. They had assumed in the early days that the plant would be 50-50 agricultural-industrial. Surprisingly, it was the industrial applications that made up the bulk of Big Quill's early business. The drywall industry uses potassium sulphate as a set accelerator. The oil industry uses it as a drilling additive.

"The industrial market has grown quickly and taken all our product," says Harvey. "In 1997 we produced 15,000 tonnes and virtually all of that went into the industrial market. We now have almost the entire drywall industry in North America."

Back in 1992, production was a more modest 3,000 tonnes, but their new ion exchange technology brought them up to the 10,000-tonne mark by 1994. The growth, of course, was gratifying. Their new ion exchange system was more efficient, but the partners soon realized that it was both too expensive and too dependent on the water levels of Big Quill Lake. In 1992, Big Quill Lake was at its lowest level ever, and during the winter it froze solid.

"So there again we had a real challenge for the company," says Harvey. "We were only nicely started and we hit a major roadblock. But we were able to find a way around it."

Harvey and his team were concerned about finding a better method of creating the product. They needed a process that would more easily accommodate continued plant expansion as markets continued to grow. There were obvious limits in using the water in Big Quill. They found their solution in glaserite technology, which, in theory, could produce potassium sulphate directly from anhydrous sodium sulphate and potash without resorting to salt water at all.

Needless to say, research and innovation have been a hallmark of the company since its inception. Earlier in its life as a privately held company, a research arm called Wynyard Technologies had been established to make herbicide additives and to do contract research to fund its own research. This sister company poured its resources into the promising glaserite process, which used anhydrous sodium sulphate to react directly with potash to create glaserite; the glaserite is then reacted with more potash to create potassium sulphate. The process itself was fairly well known, but it had never been used in commercial production.

Wynyard Technologies went through the same process that produced the ion exchange process—researching the scientific literature, creating computer models, and finally testing the concepts in a lab. In the winter of 1995 – 96, a small glaserite plant was built inside Big Quill's existing building, and by April 1996 it was in operation. Very quickly, Big Quill had another 10,000 tonnes of product from the glaserite process, in addition to the 10,000 tonnes from the ion exchange process.

The glaserite process worked so well that Big Quill Resources Inc. has invested another $3 million in an expansion that will bring it up to a total of 50,000 tonnes annually. "Our aim now is to focus on capturing more of the agriculture fertilizer market," the president reports. "Our costs of production have come down with the new technologies, and we are more competitive."

The company's five-year plan calls for another expansion to reach the 100,000 tonne level. Current sales are approaching $20 million, with projections at $70 million by 2004.

The other part of the story is *how* Big Quill made it happen. Certainly a large part of the success is owing to the leadership of Harvey Haugen, though he sees himself "as a reluctant leader and entrepreneur in some ways. I had the benefit of learning a lot about the business during my years with PCS."

Harvey, part of a large family, grew up on a farm near Birch Hills. "We were small farmers, even in those years," he remembers. "We raised about 3,000 chickens and cropped three quarters of land. Farming was always a struggle, and I was interested in how to keep the equipment going." He left the farm to complete high school at Lutheran Collegiate Bible Institute in Outlook. He took a year of Bible study, worked on the Gardiner Dam as a summer student, then completed a bachelor's degree at the University of Saskatchewan.

He got a job at Central Canada Potash in the spring of 1969 and worked his way into the position of chief chemist. Four years later he had a chance to work as a senior process engineer. In January 1979 he moved to PCS Lanigan and became involved in building an expansion to the potash refinery. His experience in the processing and business aspects of the potash industry had been rewarding and successful, but he actually resigned from the company in 1985. He was looking for something else, he says. Luckily, PCS talked him into staying, and they moved him to Wynyard in 1986 to manage the potassium sulphate pilot plant project they were starting.

"I had benefited from a series of challenging positions in the potash industry and took advantage of the career opportunities that became available," says Harvey. "You have to test the opportunities that come along. If you have not taken some opportunities early in your career you will not be able to handle the larger ones later on."

This is good advice for anyone, but particularly for budding entrepreneurs.

"My definition of success is not necessarily financial. It is the satisfaction of developing a group to work with you. I have always been very much a team player, and focused on bringing in people who were more talented than I."

Community projects require a visionary, but a well-organized team of "doers" is essential to get the job done. A major part of the success of Big Quill Resources Inc. was the belief that it could be done from within the community. Their initial success was partly a result of involving everyone in the plant in looking for improvements and innovations, and doing their research in-house in a cost-effective manner. The various building projects, whether they involved renovation or new construction, were undertaken by employees or by local contractors. The employee-owners did almost all machinery and equipment modification and maintenance. "Essentially, there is nothing we cannot do from within our community," states Harvey proudly. "Not only that, we do it better and at a lower cost."

There is no longer sufficient employment or income from 6,000-acre grain farms to sustain either families or communities. Harvey Haugen believes passionately that, "We must promote small business in all rural communities to create wealth for ourselves and our communities. Many of our employees have farm backgrounds, and our company keeps families and income in the community. We put close to $2 million in payroll alone into the local economy each year."

One of those beneficiaries is a young engineer from Wynyard. He had recently graduated from the University of Saskatchewan when Big Quill offered him his first professional job. He has since become highly skilled in building design and construction as well as in developing the processing lines.

"The key to business success is first to look on the upside of every situation," Harvey philosophizes. "We are all surrounded by opportunities. Next, you need to believe in the people you have around you. Then you need to have a good five-year plan that outlines the general direction, but focus on what needs to be done each day."

Big Quill has found that there are four aspects of the business that must always be in balance to move ahead: management capacity, technology development, available capital, and a clear marketing strategy. Big Quill has always had the capital when it was needed, largely because it has consistently taken care of the other three key aspects of business success.

"We have used this business formula ever since we started. Our management team was careful to ensure that all four components were balanced before we moved forward. But when we moved in an expansion of an existing line or the start-up of a new venture, we did it aggressively and with great confidence. And we have been successful every time."

Every time.

5

West Central Pelleting Ltd.

In 1996, the announcement that the Wilkie Hospital would be downsized to a health centre struck a devastating blow to our community. It brought more than five hundred area residents to a meeting where we aired our anger and frustration over a decision which we felt we had no hand in making.

In time, we realized the truth—that we did in fact have a hand in making that decision. Fifty years of complacency had allowed our community to shrink in population, economic viability, and regional importance. The closure of our hospital had given us a glimpse of the future...and it was not one we wanted for our children and grandchildren. Many of us felt a sense of guilt as we remembered the legacy left to us by our pioneer ancestors who settled this region with courage, optimism, creativity, innovation, and a belief they could build a better land.

— Margaret Skinner

IT was a beautiful fall day in October 1999 when over five hundred area residents gathered in the community of Wilkie for a celebration unlike any other in the history of the town. They gathered to celebrate the expansion of the shareholder-owned grain-screening pelleting plant, West Central Pelleting Ltd. (WCP); the upgrade of the United Grain Growers elevator and the opening of their new farm service centre; the opening of a new retail outlet; and the opening of the largest elk antler velveting plant in North America, Velvet Independent Processors.

The opening of the Louis Dreyfus Inland Terminal earlier in the summer, as well as the huge expansion at the Finora Canada seed-cleaning facility were also cause for celebration. Even the sting of the hospital closure had been soothed somewhat by the new health centre addition to the long-term care home and the announcement of plans to convert the former hospital building to an enriched living complex for twenty-eight residents.

This day of celebration was the culmination of four years of diversification and growth. And with the celebration came the knowledge that the community had faced the bottom of the downward spiral, made some changes, and recovered to meet the future on their own terms. In four years, the community had moved from complacency, negativity, and depression to buoyancy, confidence, and optimism.

It began with a small group of local leaders who had a vision for a better future and the courage of their convictions. Jim and Margaret Skinner were a key part of that group.

"Jim and I had farmed near Wilkie for thirty-five years and together raised three fine sons," Margaret relates. "Through the years we built a farm which was to be the future for those sons. About the time they started graduating from high school, we realized that our farm had no future for them; it was barely providing a living for us."

The Skinners encouraged their sons to go to university, and that turned out to be their first investment in agricultural diversification. In total, they "harvested" a certificate in local government administration, two School of Agriculture diplomas, one degree in Economics, two College of Agriculture degrees, and a Masters in Agricultural Economics.

The Skinners' first experience of regional economic development came through Jim's attendance at a public meeting in the neighbouring community of Unity in the mid-1990s. Area farmers had gathered to investigate the building of a producer-owned inland grain terminal. The success of a similar operation at Weyburn, not to mention years of frustration with the existing elevator system, had provided the impetus for the meeting. Jim Skinner became a director for the terminal, while Margaret volunteered to write press releases and work on developing promotional materials for what would eventually become North West Terminal.

Even before the Terminal opened, the need for a local facility to process the waste product—commonly referred to as refuse, or grain screenings—became apparent. It was an ideal spin-off industry that would enhance the bottom line for the terminal, the farmers, and other grain-cleaning facilities in the area. With the loss of the Crow freight subsidies, the futility of shipping uncleaned grain to port for export suddenly struck producers in a way they could understand—through

West Central Pelleting Ltd., in Wilkie, SK, produces grain-screenings feed pellets.

their pocketbooks—particularly when they were obliged to pick up the full costs associated with the outdated practice.

The idea for a processing facility for grain screenings was presented to the Wilkie Economic Development Board, which was looking for ways to breathe new life into the community. The board called a meeting with local municipal authorities, a highly respected consulting firm, and a solicitor. The potential and the problems were thoroughly discussed, and WCP was conceived.

"A steering committee was struck comprised of representatives of a number of communities within the area," Margaret Skinner recalls. "We worked to provide the groundwork and support for a feasibility study, and funding was provided through a campaign for donations and a matching grant from the federal-provincial Partnership for Agriculture Rural Development (PARD)."

Convincing area residents to donate a few dollars toward the $10,000 needed for the communities' share of the feasibility study was relatively easy, although there were plenty of naysayers who took pleasure in pointing out that Wilkie had never been successful with such projects in the past.

"The feasibility study was positive," says Margaret, "and on April 22, 1996 West Central Pelleting Ltd. was born. Then the campaign for the mental and financial support of our community and neighbouring communities began in earnest."

The steering committee used a number of techniques to build community support:

- A twelve-member Board of Directors was created, which included representatives of three neighbouring communities as well as the mayor and the town administrator from Wilkie;

- A slate of thirty-six promoters, or salespeople, was selected geographically to represent the twelve communities in the region;

- The new Board armed itself with competent professional advice through a solicitor and a reputable consulting firm;

- The Board began a program of public education, using public meetings and the media to educate investors and the community on the merits of grain screenings as a feed product; and

- A highly respected expert, Vern Racz, head of the Feed Resource Centre at the University of Saskatchewan, was identified as a mentor and his involvement validated the project. At fifteen public meetings throughout the region, Racz spoke on the value of grain screenings as a feed product, and his strong support of the concept gave the project a credibility that the Board alone could never have attained.

The community received additional public recognition through a newspaper column written by Kevin Hursh. "Although we did not know Kevin at the time," says Margaret, "his early recognition and endorsement of our efforts, and his subsequent presentation at a local public gathering, helped to bring credibility to the financial campaign involved with the sale of public shares."

Despite their superb organization, raising $800,000 through the sale of shares turned out to be a monumental task. The campaign lasted eighteen months. It was always difficult, and at times extremely frustrating, but no one ever suggested giving up.

"We already had an 'attitude'," Margaret laughs. "In the end, we succeeded in a community where previous attempts at projects had failed."

One of the reasons they did succeed is that they caught the imaginations of their rural supporters. To grain producers and their families, an agricultural project made perfect sense. But their urban friends also understood, perhaps because of the following analogy, which was often used to help explain the project:

> Consider for a moment an item in *Ripley's Believe It or Not* which pictures a plain bar of iron. It is valued at $5. The same bar of iron has a far different value if it is fashioned into different items. As a pair of horseshoes, it is worth $50; as sewing needles, $5,000; as balance springs for fine Swiss watches, it would be worth $500,000.

The comparison was applicable to grain screenings, which were generally considered useless refuse in Western Canada but a valued commodity on the global scene. The idea of producing a salable product from an inexpensive, readily available raw material was an attractive one, and not difficult to understand.

The success of the community-based inland terminal at Unity gave credence to the idea of regions working together for the benefit of all. One powerful negative force that had to be overcome, however, was the traditional rivalry between Wilkie and Unity. To offset possible difficulties, two Unity farmers were invited to join the project while it was still at the planning committee stage. They remained as board members, and one has served as vice-chair since those early days. The Skinners' involvement on the Board in support of the Unity Inland Terminal also helped win the support of many Unity area residents for locating the pelleting plant near Wilkie.

The fight to save the hospital had given community residents an adhesive strength they had never felt before. Locally, the steering committee built on that strength. The Board they formed earned the trust of the people who purchased the shares, and that trust was vindicated. Failure was not an option. If WCP had failed, future attempts at diversification would have been irreparably compromised.

Community leaders had the support and the assistance of the people who had built the inland terminal and the owners of grain-cleaning facilities, as well as strong support from those far-seeing individuals who could visualize the third logical step—a livestock feeding venture as part of a larger diversification plan in the region.

They chose a project that built on local strengths and advantages:

- a wide variety of crops was grown in the area;
- there was a strong and experienced agricultural work force;
- there were excellent transportation links;
- the location was central to a number of cleaning facilities;
- there was proximity to the end market.

They hired the best professional help they could get, including a competent and visionary project general manager who arrived on the scene to help design the building and has remained to guide the company through its first year of operation. This came at a significant cost, but community leaders believed it dramatically reduced the risks of the venture while at the same time improving its credibility.

The Board sold shares at low cost, allowing anyone to be a shareholder. A low share issue price may not fit every situation, but the Board believed it was the only way to light the path toward economic diversification. The cumbersome group of 500 owners in WCP became 500 cheerleaders who burst with pride when they show off their pelleting plant.

WCP was only an idea in 1996. By late 1999 it had completed its first year of full operation, which included a large expansion phase. The business produces a wide range of livestock feed products, which vary in formulation but not in consistency. Their motto is, appropriately, "As Consistent as the Rising Sun," and they intend to build and hold their market share by providing a quality assured product. Maintaining their position as an independent company creates opportunities in both the acquisition of raw materials and in the sale of their finished products. The WCP Board of Directors maintains close contact with Vern

Racz and the Prairie Feed Resource Centre at the University of Saskatchewan, and work extremely hard staying abreast of new and innovative approaches in the production and marketing of feed pellets.

When asked why this venture worked so well in a community that has faced fifty years of decline, Margaret Skinner replies, "A key reason was the extra effort we made to redefine our community more regionally." In recent years, Margaret has served as the Economic Development Consultant for the Grainland Economic Development Authority, a body made up of the towns of Wilkie and Scott and the Rural Municipalities of Reford and Buffalo. "This body works together in the recognition that what benefits one benefits all," she explains. "We had to swallow our pride, forget our fifty-year history of petty competitiveness, and learn to work together with neighbouring communities."

"In accepting the position of Economic Development Consultant," she continues, "it was my personal commitment to see three strong new agricultural based ventures come into our area to benefit each part of our broader community. This resulted in WCP, Louis Dreyfus, and Velvet Independent Processors Ltd., our own family business."

The real success has been the jobs and economic spin-offs for the local communities. Over seventy new jobs have been created in the larger community owing to the business development of the past four years, and the demand for highly educated and qualified employees has changed the face of the community. Instead of exporting their young people to high-paying jobs in the cities or out of the province, the communities in the area are now able to offer challenging positions to their children, positions that make ample use of their education.

The Skinner sons are a prime example of this phenomenon. The eldest moved back from Winnipeg in January 1999 to accept the position of general manager at North West Terminal in Unity. The second son is general manager of Velvet Independent Processors in Wilkie. The youngest son is making his living in Saskatoon as a consultant on community projects, including inland terminals, hog barns, and grain screenings pelleting plants.

The return of their sons has been a source of great satisfaction for Jim and Margaret Skinner. At the turn of the millennium, this is the way farm families and rural businesses will keep their children in the community; they will be active in family businesses, strengthening and rebuilding rural Saskatchewan.

The seventy-five new jobs in Wilkie have inevitably attracted other young people to the community. Young people bring young families. Young families strengthen the school systems, sports and cultural activities, and the general infrastructure and services provided in the community.

According to Margaret Skinner, though, they're just getting started: "The early success has been sweet, but we know we must keep working, as the world is a rapidly changing place. We realize that our future competitive advantage is our attitude. We now know that we can do anything, and that has made all the difference."

6

Kitsaki Management Limited Partnership

Early in 1980 the Lac La Ronge Band Council met to determine the future of their community. They realized that their reliance on the federal government was destroying both their society and their economy. They needed to develop business ventures that provided employment opportunities for First Nations people. But they had few resources, and no means of accessing investment or loan capital.

In a bold move they formed the Kitsaki Development Corporation, an earlier name, a commercial entity that could borrow money against its collateral like any business venture off the reserve. They contracted a non-First Nations manager and accountant to assist in the operation of the corporation.

Twenty years later, Kitsaki has become one of the best examples of community-based economic development in the province. The band of 7,000 First Nations people owns or jointly owns thirty companies and twelve businesses, including a hotel, catering companies that service the northern forest and mining industry, a food processing plant, and many other ventures. Pro-rated sales for the year ending March 2000 exceeded $21 million. Kitsaki has also been an innovative leader in developing education and training programs for band members.

IN September 1999, Chief Harry Cook made a passionate appeal to the Saskatchewan business community. "I believe that there are always business opportunities available, and it is up to us to take advantage of those opportunities," he said. "But it is also in the best interest of the non-First Nations governments and business community to co-operate with us, so we can make sure our growing population becomes an important segment of Saskatchewan's workforce."

The Chief of the Lac La Ronge Indian Band was thinking of a recent study that predicted the First Nations population of Saskatchewan would triple over the next fifty years, to 350,000. Unfortunately, the unemployment rate was also predicted to increase—from fifty-three percent today to eighty-three percent by 2050.

"We must try to grow our own businesses to make sure that these gloomy projections do not happen," Chief Cook stated simply.

Harry Cook, now fifty-seven years old, was raised in Stanley Mission on the Churchill River in northern Saskatchewan. He worked with his parents, traditional trappers and fishermen, until he was sent away to school in Prince Albert at the age of nine. He was sixteen when he finished grade eight and returned to Stanley Mission to take up a traditional lifestyle. But in the 1950s it was becoming increasingly difficult to earn even a subsistence living, and Harry was soon back in Prince Albert, enrolled in high school as a mature student. After completing grade ten, he trained as a welder at the Kelsey Campus of the Saskatchewan Institute of Applied Arts and Sciences in Saskatoon. Once certified, he was hired by Westeel Rosco in Regina, a fast-growing enterprise that later became Westank Willock Company. He worked there for the next thirteen years building grain bins and fuel tanks, and incidentally observing first-hand what was required to build a small business into a large business.

With his wife, Rose, and their two daughters, he spent two of his three weeks annual vacation up north every year. Rose was from La Ronge, and they both still considered the north their home. As the years passed in Regina, they found themselves missing it more and more, until they finally decided to move back.

Harry had bought a number of rental houses in Regina. It was those investments, together with their savings, that allowed the family to settle in La Ronge and take their time about deciding what to do. They had been back home for almost a year when the band offered Harry the position of Co-ordinator of Band Housing. It was a position for which he was uniquely qualified, having been a landlord for years in Regina. He served in various other positions on the Band Council as well, until in 1987 he was elected Chief. He is now in his sixth term, which will expire in 2002. In addition to his administrative duties on the Band Council, he sits on the Board of Directors of Cameco, the Federation of Saskatchewan Indian Nations, and a number of other organizations.

"Aboriginal people must take the initiative to develop businesses for our own benefit," he states, "or others will do it for theirs. We have everything to gain by taking action and everything to lose if we do not. This is not a hard thing to understand."

Harry's vision goes back to the late 1970s when Chief Myles Venne and the La Ronge Band Council were beginning to recognize that economic development was a concern they needed to address. Unless the band was involved in a project, they had noticed, band members seldom got any jobs from it. At the time, there were some federal funds allocated to bands so that they might take responsibility for their own social, health, and education programs, but that rarely translated into jobs. "We needed to get into some kind of business ventures to create opportunities for training and employment," Harry recalls.

It was obvious to Chief Venne that northern development was accelerating, and all kinds of business opportunities were becoming available. The band had better take some ownership, he thought, if they wanted to guide the development of the north in a way that benefited northern communities and was not harmful to the environment.

They started out by failing, which is only a bad thing in business if you never try again. It was from of the ashes of that original failure that the Kitsaki Development Corporation rose in the early 1980s.

It started with the Key Lake Mining Corporation, which was looking for northern partners for joint ventures. Government regulations gave ten percent preference to northern businesses interested in bidding on construction contracts, and Key Lake was ideally situated for joint ventures as it began work on a new mine. Merriman Transport was joint-ventured with the Lac La Ronge band to provide crushed aggregates to the mine site. The company successfully bid for the contract, but when the band approached the bank in mid-1981 to borrow money for the project, they were informed that the band was not "a person at law." They could not, therefore, borrow money.

Taking legal advice, they decided to form a limited company, with shares owned by the band members and held in trust by the Chief. The result was that on December 14, 1981 Kitsaki Development Corporation was formed to finance Merriman Transport. The band hired a professional manager and completed the

The Lac La Ronge Indian Band Chief and Council, from left to right: Councillor Leonard P. Venne, Hall Lake; Councillor Sam Halkett, Little Red River; Councillor Keith Mirasty, Little Red River; Councillor Kenny Ratt, Sucker River; Councillor Tammy Cook-Searson, La Ronge; Councillor Gordon Hardlotte, Stanley Mission; Councillor Bernice Roberts, Stanley Mission; Treaty Land Entitlement Lawyer, Gary Nelson, Vancouver; Chief Harry Cook; Treaty Land Entitlement Lawyer, Thomas Berger, Vancouver; Elder Catherine Charles, La Ronge; Councillor Rodney Hegland, La Ronge; Senator Myles Venne, Councillor Jimmy Roberts, La Ronge; Councillor Lester Roberts, Stanley Mission. Missing: Councillor William G. Roberts, La Ronge; Councillor Leon Charles, Grandmothers Bay; Elder Doris Halkett, Little Red River; Elder Peter Roberts, Stanley Mission; Elder Elizabeth Charles, Stanley Mission.

Key Lake contract. Once the mining contract was complete, however, they found themselves with neither the resources nor the skills to move ahead, despite numerous opportunities.

Band leaders were not discouraged. If business development were to continue—and they were convinced that it should—they knew they had to acquire business expertise to meet their objectives. It was an important lesson, one that led them eventually to meet with Trimac Transport. That resulted in Northern Resource Trucking, which has since earned a well-deserved reputation as a successful and stable Native-owned corporation. With Northern Resource Trucking (NRT) as a cornerstone, Kitsaki developed a number of business enterprises in a range of sectors. NRT reorganized in 1995 to include eight other First Nations as equity partners, including:

- Peter Ballantyne Cree Nation;
- Montreal Lake Cree Nation;

- Denesuline Development Corporation (Hatchet Lake, Black Lake, and Fond du Lac First Nations);

- Clearwater River Dene Nation;

- English River First Nation;

- Cumberland House Cree Nation; Northern Village of Cumberland House;

- Northern Village of Ile-à-la-Crosse;

- Northern Village of Buffalo Narrows.

Kitsaki now has subsidiary companies with investments in virtually all sectors of the regional economy.

"One of the reasons for our success," according to Chief Harry Cook, "is that Kitsaki wants to manage a group of companies rather than individual companies. We attempt to obtain ownership positions in firms where the management in place are highly motivated entrepreneurs, or a strong corporate partner. We look at business deals in terms, first, of profits; second, participation in management through ownership; and third, employment."

Partnerships with non-First Nations firms have allowed Kitsaki to secure competent management personnel during the planning, start-up, and initial operation phase of a business venture, and have provided valuable opportunities for band members to be trained to assume increasingly responsible positions. "We are very happy when we have a band member who is qualified to manage one of our businesses," says Harry. "But if we need to employ non-band members to make a business a success, we will do that, too."

Kitsaki business investments currently include partnerships with a number of First Nations and non-First Nations firms, including:

- *Wapawekka Lumber Limited Partnership*. A partnership with the Peter Ballantyne Cree Nation, the Montreal Lake Cree Nation, and Weyerhaeuser, Wapawekka started production in the spring of 1999 and employs about forty-five highly skilled technical people.

- *Northern Resource Trucking*. This partnership includes a dozen different Indian and Métis communities across Northern Saskatchewan as well as Trimac Transportation, one of the largest bulk haulers in North America. NRT employs approximately 100 people and does most of the bulk hauling for Cameco and Cogema.

- *Athabasca Catering Limited Partnership*. A partnership between four other First Nations and Kitsaki and private Saskatoon entrepreneurs, Athabasca Catering performs food service and janitorial work at four different uranium mine sites operated by Cameco in northern Saskatchewan. It employs about 150 people.

- *La Ronge Motor Hotel*. Kitsaki is the sole owner of the only full-service hotel in La Ronge, employing on the average seventy-five full-time and part-time people.

- *Kitsaki Meats*. Kitsaki is also the sole owner of this meat snack company that produces products for Mitchell's Gourmet Foods and Westfair's Superstore as well as markets in Ontario. The company employs fifteen people; it is currently introducing a new product combining their excellent sausage with organically grown wild rice, and has become a major exporter of wild rice.

- *La Ronge Industries*. One of the largest growers of wild rice in Canada, LRI builds on the historical agriculture of the Woodland Cree.

- *First Nations Insurance Services*. These services began as an insurance broker to provide group pension and benefits to First Nations and their organizations. Kitsaki currently owns this business venture in conjunction with the Peter Ballantyne Cree Nation and the Federation of Saskatchewan Indian Nations.

- *Keewatin Mining*. A partnership that includes the Athabasca First Nations, performs contract mining services for the mining industry in Saskatchewan, joint venturing with Procon Mining and Tunneling.

- *Canada North Environmental Services Limited Partnership*. This is a new partnership with Connor Pacific, doing environmental monitoring work and related activities.

- *Woodland Cree Resources*. This is a partnership between Montreal Lake and Peter Ballantyne, and performs wood harvesting activities for Weyerhaeuser.

- *Dakota Winds Kitsaki*. The newest partnership, Dakota Winds is a mechanical services business headquartered in Saskatoon, with a new office in La Ronge. It was started by the Whitecap Dakota First Nation as a joint venture with Inter-City Mechanical in Saskatoon.

- *The Prince Albert Inn, the Marlboro Inn, and the Marquis Inn*. These three Prince Albert hotels are each partially owned by the Lac La Ronge Indian Band as a result of their participation in the Prince Albert Grand Council.

"As you can see," says Chief Cook. "we consider partnerships to be an important element of our future. Economic development is long term; successful businesses are not built in a few short months. It takes years to build them up." While the co-operation of business and governments has been instrumental in creating a good business climate for First Nations, it has been more important "to constantly remind ourselves that, as political leaders, it is up to us to have a long-term vision for a growing, healthy First Nations business sector. But it is not our place, as politicians, to manage those businesses. That we must leave to the business managers."

Currently, there are about 500 people working for the Kitsaki Management Limited Partnership companies. Approximately one-third are from the Lac La Ronge band, one-third from other First Nations, and one-third are non-First Nations. The level of education among First Nations is low, and many people have limited work experience, but the challenge of preparing First Nations people for employment is one of the main reasons Kitsaki was started in the first place.

Lacking the economic benefits of oil, natural gas, or treaty land entitlements, the La Ronge band has achieved its success on the strength of northern people understanding the value of the human and natural resources that are available in their communities.

The future is bright. The current CEO, Ray McKay, a member of the Lac La Ronge Indian Band, was also raised on a trapline along the Churchill River. He left the north to obtain an education, then embarked on a prestigious career that included positions as a teacher, assistant principal, principal, and executive director of Northern Education Services in La Ronge. He was a member of the Canadian delegation to the 41st International Conference on Education in Geneva and helped initiate the Northern Education Task Force in 1989. He retired as Deputy Minister of Northern Affairs for the Government of Saskatchewan in 1998 to return home and join Kitsaki as Chief Executive Officer. "One of the reasons for Kitsaki's growth was the effort by the Province of Saskatchewan to foster a good business climate for northern aboriginal business," states Ray McKay; "successful economic development must be driven by entrepreneurs but government must also provide a supportive business climate."

Chief Harry Cook credits his own success to a balanced life: "My priority is my wife and kids. It is easier to deal with issues with a loving and caring home. This gives me the energy and ability to care for others." Similarly, "In order to have a good society, we must have stable and healthy families. Broken homes provide little guidance and direction for our young. This is part of my leadership approach and vision for the future for all Saskatchewan people!"

Group Ventures

7

Lakeside Machinery Co-operative Ltd.

Listen to any group of farmers and they will give you an earful on low grain prices, high machinery costs, uncertain markets, and, if there is even a future for agriculture, how to get their children involved in the family business. This may sound very current, but they were the same issues farmers were voicing across Saskatchewan thirty years ago. In 1971, a group of small farmers in the Dafoe area decided to work together to deal with these challenges. The result, Lakeside Machinery Co-operative Ltd., is a multi-million dollar venture that has diversified to Lakeside Seeds Ltd., Lakeside Processors Ltd., and, most recently, Lakeside Pulse and Special Crops Ltd.

LAKESIDE got its start in 1970 – 71 during years of low prices and declining markets. A group of seven farmers, realizing that they would soon be facing financial trouble if they did not take some creative action, particularly with their old farm equipment, formed a machinery co-operative in an attempt to meet their mutual needs.

The seven founders were all in their fifties when they started and wise enough to know that they needed expert advice. They spent time with a lawyer, an accountant, and the Department of Co-operatives. The start-up process took a year and the start-up costs were high, but they judged it worth the expense to establish the business properly.

For the first few years Lakeside operated a out of a member's yard. In 1976 they bought land and built a shop for maintenance and storage. Expanding the original intent of the co-op, they bought an old elevator annex along the Yellowhead Highway near Kandahar to increase their grain storage, drying, and handling capacity. With a newly installed leg and dryer, this facility was central to the operation for many years.

In 1979 the co-op grew its first field of pedigreed seed, a venture which led to the formation of Lakeside Seeds and the construction of a seed-cleaning facility. Lakeside Seeds, a registered business name, is not a separate entity but part of Lakeside Machinery Co-operative Ltd. They began growing lentils in 1980, followed by peas, mustard, and other specialty crops such as coriander. Developing an export market for their specialty crops eventually grew into Lakeside Processors and a separate facility on the CP rail line at Dafoe, a joint venture with the Saskatchewan Wheat Pool.

Lakeside was founded under the Co-operative Act; it operates as a co-operative, but is taxed as a small business corporation. A true co-operative would pay out its equity, but Lakeside has determined that a corporate business structure has more advantages from a tax point of view. Lakeside pays corporate tax each year, and individual members of the co-operative pay income tax. Each member builds equity in the corporation, contributing to their buy-out on retirement.

Other machinery co-operatives in Saskatchewan work on a simpler basis. Lakeside's more formal structure, however, has allowed for the successful transition of the business to a second generation—the current five member-families are all descendants of the original seven—and has also laid the foundation for diversification and expansion into other ventures. For example, Lakeside has jointly owned export trading companies that have helped to develop direct-market links to specific customers around the world, which is something individual farmers or even more traditional co-operatives could never have done on their own. But Lakeside had the organizational structure to do it.

"We have not expanded our land base for the past ten years," says Glen Laxdal, one of the current members. "Instead, we have invested our capital in the seed plant and in other value-added business ventures such as Lakeside Processors Ltd."

This latter venture was conceived in 1991 to meet the demands of the growing export market. In 1993 the Saskatchewan Wheat Pool announced that it was closing the Dafoe elevator. When Lakeside approached them about buying it, the Pool responded with the offer of a joint venture. This resulted in the formation of Lakeside Processors and the construction of a \$2.1 million processing facility beside the Pool elevator. Lakeside Ventures is the majority shareholder, with a sixty-five percent interest, while the Wheat Pool holds the remainder. The plant is run by an independent manager who supervises twelve to fifteen employees.

The rail line beside the facility has room for twenty-eight cars. With the capacity to process and load eighteen cars a week, Lakeside Processors are busy all year.

Over the past five years, Lakeside has not had to chase any new business. The development of value-added processing in the early 1990s combined with a well-planned domestic and export marketing program has kept them at full capacity. Like all successful entrepreneurs, however, they are keeping one eye on the future. They have plans to expand their trading operations to take advantage of niche markets in the export trade.

The five current members of the co-operative focus on their business partnership, and do not socialize much as a group. At one point they were all neighbours, but their individual home sites have now broadened to include Wynyard. The members have intentionally spread themselves throughout their communities, serving variously on the boards of the local credit union and retail co-operative, Ducks Unlimited, the seed growers, school boards, the golf and country club, the curling club, the Chamber of Commerce, and numerous other community groups. It is part of their business plan that they be perceived as improving the quality of life in the community.

One of the members, Wayne Blyth, has a diploma in Agriculture from the University of Saskatchewan, but the rest have only high school education. Many of their predecessors had less than that. But ordinary farmers can do extraordinary things by working together, and the generations have learned as they went. They stay ahead of agricultural trends by subscribing to a range of farm and business magazines, attending conferences, and keeping an eye on the markets.

Their original method of business management has been carried forward to the present. The current five members own about the same amount of land—a total of 6,000 cultivated acres—that is managed as a single farm. The grain is pooled. Labour, expenses, and revenue are shared according to the land equity base. Everyone keeps daily timesheets. At the end of the month, hours are tallied. If any member is under the running average, he pays those who were over the average on the basis of $10 per hour.

Everyone is directly involved in seeding, harvest, and seasonal busy periods such as rouging (removing undesirable plants) the pedigreed seed fields. "We run teams in shifts in the spring with two large air seeders, and during harvest with two large combines," says Glen Laxdal. "Together we can seed 6,000 acres as fast as one farmer can seed 1,000 on his own, which takes us about eighteen days."

Left to right: Glen Bolt, Greg Blyth, Dan Blyth, Glen Laxdal and Wayne Blyth are the owners of Lakeside Machinery Co-operative Ltd., in Dafoe, SK.

The members specialize in different areas. Indeed, diversity of interests is one of the keys to their success. Glen Laxdal, for instance, is the grain trader. Glen Bolt runs the seed plant, and is also responsible for the grain cleaning, storage, and shipping. Wayne Blyth is the bookkeeper, farm manager, and general co-ordinator. Greg Blyth concentrates his energies on repair and maintenance, while Dan Blyth is responsible for the grain hauling with the semi. Everyone is constantly stepping outside his own area to help the others, though, because each recognizes that the success of each unit is part of the success of the whole business. There is no organizational hierarchy, with one person acting as leader. Everyone is equal. There is a president, but that is a position only; everyone is part of the decision-making process. No work is deemed more important than any other.

A clear vision and common goals are critical to the success of the business. This can only be accomplished through communication. The members meet formally once a month, but during busy times they meet once a week, or even daily, to make sure that everything is going smoothly. Business goals are established at the annual meeting, and the operating principles for implementation are outlined in the bylaws.

The benefits of membership in the co-operative are numerous. They share the work load and, thus, the stress. They are able to diversify, to take on new ventures, with lower risk. And they have an excellent means of involving the next generation in the farm business. But one of the major benefits remains the original one: machinery.

"Our machinery investment per acre for equipment is about one-half that of a conventional farmer," says Laxdal. Lakeside's equipment is new and state-of-the-art. There is no downtime during the critical seeding and harvest seasons.

Another benefit is the maximum use of labour. By each of the members finding an area that fits his skills and interests, they have dramatically increased their labour efficiency. "It has a synergistic effect," says Laxdal philosophically. "Five working together are much more effective than five working alone. We work in shifts. Some of us are the early birds and like to start work at 4:00 or 5:00 a.m. Others like to start later in the day but can work late into the night." An added bonus is that members can schedule vacation time with their families, knowing that the operation will remain in good hands while they are away. They all make a good income from the farm, and none of their families has to rely on off farm income.

It is the diversification ventures resulting in Lakeside Seeds and Lakeside Processors that have provided the real wealth within the co-op. "The bulk of our income," Laxdal states, "comes from value-added businesses, and we are no longer dependent on commodity crops. For example, we grew 500 acres of coriander. We buy and sell peas and lentils for cleaning, processing, and export. About one-half of the land base is in pedigreed seed production. In total, we have assets of $3.5 million, not including land. This is the reason why our farm income is no longer dependent on the yields and quality of our own crops."

One of the objectives of the seven founders was to be able to transfer the farm to the next generation in a manner the children could afford and yet still provide some equity for the parents. The first inter-generation transfer has worked extremely well, and the co-operative is now nearing the stage that a third generation is considering entering the business. The procedures for them to do this have been tested and found effective.

According to Glen Laxdal, the members are often asked about the downside of operating a co-operative farm. "None of us know any other structure," he replies, "since all of us were brought into the business at a young age by our fathers. I think our fathers found it hard at times. Decision-making can be very slow and cumbersome. The group must be committed to open communication."

That doesn't mean that the members always agree, he hastens to add. "Sometimes one or two members don't agree on a decision, but the majority still rules. Major purchasing decisions, however, are usually decided by unanimous consent. There have also been times when members left the co-op, but in those cases the partings have been amicable."

The secret of the original seven members' success with Lakeside was their willingness to take responsibility for their situation. They were not afraid to take action and plan their own future. Thirty years later, the challenges facing farmers appear even greater, with declining commodity prices, high machinery costs, changing markets, and the constant need to integrate the next generation into the farm economy.

Given today's rapidly changing business and marketing environment, there has been considerable discussion about the development of corporate farms. Lakeside has all the features of a multi-million-dollar business but it still remains in the control of small farmers, who each own about 1,200 acres of their own land that makes up the larger farm unit. Diversification and value-added ventures have insulated the farm from fluctuating commodity prices. From a management point of view, their achievements have been outstanding. But success has not occurred by accident.

On a purely practical level, based on the experience of the original seven members, it is apparent that anyone starting up a co-operative should first establish a formal structure. This will require some resources, including lawyers and accountants. It is best to start with a shareholder agreement and a good set of by-laws. There must be provisions for valuation, how to buy into the business, and how to get out. The co-operative must clearly stipulate what members own individually and what they own jointly. These must all be in place before the co-operative commences operations, otherwise problems will arise in the future.

With these issues in mind, the co-op continues to reinvent itself. Up to December 1999, the group had marketed all their products through Lakeside Seeds. As the business grew, however, the responsibilities became too much for the five owners. In January, 2000, a new company was formed, Lakeside Pulse and Special Crops Ltd. Based in Winnipeg, it is owned by the five co-op members plus Cam Laxdal, Glen's brother. Cam had been working in agricultural marketing in Winnipeg, and became the manager of the new company, whose role was to take responsibility for marketing all of Lakeside's seed and pulse processing plus those of other pulse and specialty crop processors across western Canada.

"We had successfully developed more markets than we could fill on our own," says Glen, "so it made sense to develop a marketing company. More importantly, we did not want to create a single large company that we couldn't sell or transfer to the next generation."

This leaves Lakeside Machinery Co-op the farm management group, which has a mechanism to bring in the next generation of farmers while the present owners stay involved as equity shareholders in the other two companies. Any one of the three businesses can be sold without affecting the viability of the other ventures.

Lakeside Machinery Co-operative Ltd. works because the members have been able to communicate the shared vision they inherited from their fathers. They get along together. They make sure that everyone understands how the co-op works and how the dollars come and go. And they are willing to channel their diverse skills into specific areas of expertise for the good of the whole company.

In a nutshell, the lessons to be learned from this business venture are:

- Develop a common vision;
- Share the vision and develop a common mission;
- Do your homework;
- Use legal and financial experts;
- Take advantage of government services and support;
- Communicate, communicate, communicate.

Above all, recognize that people are *the* most valuable resource. Through identifying individual strengths, Lakeside Machinery Co-operative Ltd. has for two generations been able to accomplish more as a team than they ever could have individually.

8

Delsa Food Processors Inc.

The imminent demise of the Crow rate in the late 1980s saw some farmers tearing their hair and stamping their feet, others preparing to give in and sell up, and others looking for alternatives. One of the more successful alternatives turned out to be Delsa Food Processors Inc. Delsa—its name is a combination of "Delisle" and "Saskatchewan," where the plant is located—produces more than ten tonnes of fresh salads and prepared vegetables every day for markets from Winnipeg to Vancouver. Using as much Saskatchewan-grown produce as possible, the corporation is one hundred percent locally owned, with a workforce of thirty local people who have a dramatic impact on the local economy in wages alone.

THE idea of Delsa began taking shape in 1988 when consultant Paul Melin approached the mayor of Delisle with the idea of building a mustard processing plant. The idea made sense; Saskatchewan is one of the world's largest producers of condiment-quality mustard seed, and most of it is exported to Europe for processing and marketing.

Ten local residents attended a meeting to explore the idea. Nine of the ten were grain farmers who knew they could not survive much longer by growing wheat alone. With an initial investment from each of them, the group was able to take advantage of matching government funds through a business development program and hired Paul Melin to conduct a feasibility study.

Paul went to Holland to conduct his initial research into the production, processing, and marketing opportunities for Canadian mustard. While there, he became acquainted with Smilde, a huge, family owned company that manufactures prepared salads and processed meats out of several factories. The Dutch entrepreneurs were drawn to Paul because of his Canadian background, and they were happy to take the time to explain their business to him. Paul was impressed with what he saw. On an impulse, he asked the owner if Smilde would be interested in a joint venture with a Canadian company. The owner was intrigued.

Paul returned to Canada with a discouraging report about the economic viability of processing condiment mustard in Saskatchewan. The European market would be too difficult to break into, he thought. The competition was intense, the margins thin. The volume of sales would likely be too low to justify the costs of a processing plant in Delisle. He did, however, have something to say about the huge potential for prepared salads in the western Canadian market. Given the town's proximity to the Outlook irrigation districts, Delisle would be an ideal location for such a business. He encouraged the investment group to visit Holland with him and see for themselves what Smilde had accomplished.

Three members of the group went to Holland with Paul. They came away deeply impressed with Smilde's creative technologies in salad preparation, packaging, and handling. Using only fresh ingredients and natural preservatives, the Dutch company was able to market "fresh" salads with an impressive twenty-eight-day shelf life.

Four months later, after some competent and necessary research into the feasibility of the salad industry, Delsa was born as a joint venture with local investors and Smilde. The Delisle group formed a holding company that owned fifty-one percent of Delsa; the Dutch company owned the remaining forty-nine. Delsa Food Processors Inc. held its grand opening in June 1989.

The first year was almost a disaster. Smilde, without informing its Canadian partner, had altered its recipes to suit Canadian tastes before handing them over to Delsa. Smilde's idea of Canadian tastes, unfortunately, differed from that of most Canadians, and Delsa was mystified at the difficulties they were having with the quality and taste of their product. Ironically, it was the Dutch production foreman that Smilde sent from Holland to assist its new Canadian partner who discovered that the recipes Delsa was using were not the same as Smilde's European version.

It was a year before they could correct the quality to their satisfaction and establish a marketing and distribution system. During that time, sales were poor, and the $300,000 Delsa plant was forced to produce an array of other products, including pizzas, to keep the production lines going and produce a much-needed cash flow.

Owing to the initial troubles, the Dutch investors lost interest in the venture and offered their shares to the Canadians. In a reversal of the usual scenario, in

Syd Hill takes a break from processing salad at Delsa Food Processors Inc., in Delisle, SK.

which small companies typically merge with bigger ones to access a larger market or to secure the quality of their supplies, Delsa was soon owned entirely by local investors. Of the twenty-five shareholders, twenty-two live locally. One of the "outside" shareholders lives in Saskatoon; the other two live in Calgary. When the business was struggling, each shareholder was required to supply personal guarantees. "When it's your cash on the line," one of them remarked, "it pushes you to try harder, to make sure you succeed."

One of the buy-out conditions was an intensive training program for Delsa Food Processors Inc. staff in salad preparation techniques based on consumer market research. It was this training that allowed the company to develop its own salads and set its own high standards for quality control. With a well-trained staff and products more suited to western Canadian tastes, Delsa began an aggressive marketing campaign, based largely on taste sampling. Based on the quality of its product, the company began supplying Price Club in Regina (which later became Costco) as well as Costco stores in Saskatoon and Winnipeg.

Delsa's big break came in 1994 when KFC Restaurants embarked on a program to standardize taste and quality in all their outlets. Eastern Canadian KFC outlets were already serving prepared salads manufactured by a single company. Looking for options, KFC investigated Delsa as well as another prepared salad company in Edmonton. Delsa was awarded the contract, largely owing to the quality control standards they had developed with the Dutch. The Delisle company was soon supplying Saskatoon and Regina KFC restaurants with a full range of prepared salads. A year later, Winnipeg and Edmonton outlets were added to the Delsa roster.

Then KFC asked Delsa to supply its restaurants in British Columbia. With only two weeks lead time, Delsa moved from producing two tonnes of salad per day to five. The transition was not as smooth as everyone would have liked. Delsa was constantly running short of supplies, but KFC was willing to accept some delays as long as the Saskatchewan company continued to deliver the same consistent quality and taste to every outlet.

Today, Delsa produces five varieties of salads—macaroni, potato, potato and egg, coleslaw, and pasta—and employs thirty-five people, thirty of whom are local; the others commute daily from Saskatoon. During the summer, when the plant operates two shifts, Delsa brings in student labour. The community is supportive of the economic prosperity Delsa has brought to Delisle.

Delsa Food Processors Inc. has been profitable for the past four years. A recent $200,000 expansion will eventually double production capacity and streamline the packaging area. With their new systems in place, Delsa has expanded into the prepared vegetable market, filling a tremendous consumer need.

"Your business is only as good as your employees," according to Syd Hill, one of the original members of the group, and president of the company. "We credit the success of Delsa to the employees. Delsa pays well above minimum wage and treats its employees with dignity and respect. As an example, we hired a mentally challenged individual and took extra time to train him. The efforts paid off, and the employee is now a loyal and efficient member of the Delsa team."

One of the original goals in forming the company was to create a business that would benefit the town of Delisle and its people. Many towns, however, are not prepared to welcome a large, new business to the community. Although Delsa's relationship with the community has generally been good, there have also been times of stress. In one instance, there were complaints about the odour from Delsa's lagoon. Dealing with tonnes of organic matter and thousands of litres of water every day is bound to produce a certain amount of waste, which, in turn, decomposes and begins to smell. Delsa worked with the community to solve the problem in a manner that benefited everyone.

"Everyone has to make an effort to support a major business in a small community," says Syd. "We were very lucky to get the support we did."

There are other challenges to running a large and profitable business in a small town. Labour and raw materials are not always readily available. Fortunately, the company has found people who are willing to drive out from Saskatoon every day to fill the labour gap. Occasionally, however, it has been forced to import cabbage from as far away as Holland as there was not enough product available for purchase in the United States. Syd would like to see more farmers in the area become involved in irrigation, so the vegetables for the salads could all be grown locally.

"Many people tell us that Delsa shouldn't be in Delisle," says Syd. "It should be in some place like Calgary. That may be true for some industries, but we have certainly proved that we can do it from here."

For budding entrepreneurs, Syd has some advice: "Know what you're doing before you start. If you prepare studies, make sure the consultant tells you what you need to hear, not than what you want to hear."

The key to Delsa's success was determination: "The local investors simply would not accept that the venture could not be successful. We did whatever we could and whatever was required to keep the doors open and look for solutions. At one time our only source of income was making pizzas and boxing chocolates."

The tenacity of the local investors has paid off. The future in vegetable processing looks great.

9

Rose Bush Acres

Rose Bush Acres is a unique bed and breakfast located near Watson in the heart of the prairies. Rose Bush Manor, an eighty-year-old Victorian home, is the centrepiece of an early Saskatchewan farmyard motif.

"We had a dream for a country estate vacation farm to draw people to the Watson community as a destination tourist attraction," says Colleen Haussecker. "We talked about it with Marty and June Draude for years, but had no money set aside or a real plan." They got further than the talking phase when they bought seven acres of campsite property from the town of Watson in 1990, but they just cut the grass for three years while they cruised the countryside looking for the ideal house.

Then one day, in the fall of 1992, they heard of the perfect house on CBC news. The news story was a plea for help to save a Victorian manor that had been vandalized. The Draudes and Colleen and her husband, Randy, were instantly into the venture with a series of decisions that had to be made without much thought or planning. "We were flying by the seat of our pants!" Colleen recalls.

COLLEEN and Randy Haussecker and Martin and June Draude had a vision of recreating a turn-of-the-century farm in Watson that would build a viable business and draw bird watchers, hunters, golfers, fishermen, and other tourists to the community while offering rural serenity in one of the most beautiful locations in Saskatchewan.

A September 1992 CBC television news story was of a Saskatchewan man who had purchased a stately old home in Cupar and moved it onto a site near Fort Qu'Appelle, overlooking Pasqua Lake. The man had wanted to turn the home into a bed and breakfast establishment but did not have the resources to finish the project. In the meantime, the magnificent old home had fallen victim to serious vandalism.

The Haussеckers and the Draudes drove down to Fort Qu'Appelle to see the home. After their first visit, a number of things became clear. The house was ideal for their dream, but the project was much bigger than the four of them could manage. It was equally obvious that if the house was not moved immediately, vandals would render it worthless within weeks.

"We had little time for thought during these first few weeks," says Colleen Haussecker. "Initially, we intended to run the business on our own, but now we needed an organizational structure to raise capital and bring in other shareholders."

After the initial viewing of the manor, a flurry of organizational meetings ensued. These meetings were to advertise the project to Watson people and urge then to invest their time and money. At the same time, the group hired a guard to stay in the manor at Fort Qu'Appelle and prevent further damage. Within two weeks they had attracted thirty-five investors and raised $60,000 to buy the manor as well as move it to their location.

"During that hectic period we had to make a hundred decisions a day," Colleen remembers. "But that got us to the starting point where the work really started."

They got the manor to the new location and left it on blocks while they dug a basement. By late 1992 they were rushing to get the house on its foundation and started restoration before winter set in.

A feature stained glass window was missing from the upstairs landing. Through a series of unusual circumstances, it was found in a Regina pawnshop. This was a blessing in disguise, as the theft had saved it from being vandalized. The restoration work was complicated by the fact that all the windows had to be changed, and the home featured imported wood that was different in each room. So busy were the shareholders that fall it wasn't until winter set in that they had time to look at the organizational structure for their new venture.

The group started with a corporate business structure in order to create an organization that recognized the unique contributions, both cash and in-kind, of the community shareholders. But a corporation with widely held shareholders did not fit well with the Saskatchewan Securities Commission. After some thought, a co-operative model was investigated.

"We ended up with an innovative co-operative model that allowed us to do the things we needed in terms of raising cash, building equity, and getting the job done," says Marty Draude. "But we were not a normal co-op. We wanted a $2,500 investment per person or family unit. The membership fee was $1,700 with another eighty Class A shares that could be purchased over two years. Members had the option of purchasing their Class A shares by cash, product or service, or eighty hours of sweat equity at $10 per hour. In some cases, we accepted the entire $2,500 in sweat equity for services from architects, lawyer, utilities, and landscaping." What struck them most was the vast amount of knowledge expertise that existed within the small community. Literally everything they needed was available locally.

The result was the Rose Bush Acres Heritage Resort Co-operative Ltd., legally christened in the spring of 1993. "Just as the original co-operatives brought people together at the turn of the century," Colleen recalls, "this new twist will help build new and innovative rural ventures in Saskatchewan as it heads into the new millennium."

Rose Bush Acres made money during the first year of operation and has been profitable every year since. The business has been internally financed, with only a small external debt, employing five full-time staff and five part-time staff for nine months of the year.

"Not everyone would invest in this type of enterprise," says Marty Draude. "Most of our members were not wealthy, but our member and shareholder concept allowed them to be active as investors and participate in maintaining the business. This concept worked very well in rural Saskatchewan where not everyone has extra cash laying around."

A twelve-person Board of Directors ran the co-operative, meeting every two months, while Colleen did the day-to-day decision-making. There was no question that she was the driving force behind the venture. Before Rose Bush Acres got started, she ran a hairdressing salon in Watson and managed the SARCAN recycling centre. She was involved in a regional pilot waste disposal and recycling initiative, REACT, and active on the Town Council. Her community and business experience confirmed the need for more economic activity in the surrounding region if local communities were to survive.

The idea of making Watson, Saskatchewan a tourist destination was a bold one. But when they thought about it, they realized that they had many strengths to build on. There were a number of golf courses in the area, as well as other tourist locations such as House of Treasurers in Annaheim. Excellent game and bird populations would attract hunters in the fall, and nearby Big Quill Lake had recently received funding as a bird sanctuary, so there was something for bird watchers as well. In addition to these local attractions, there was a growing demand for unique

Rose Bush Acres Bed & Breakfast near Watson, SK. Photo: Bruce Hobin.

locations for small conventions, corporate planning, country weddings, and country "getaways."

"You must have a vision and not veer off that vision," says Colleen when asked about the key factors in their success. "You must be prepared to finance the venture yourself. Even if it is community based and financed, the leaders must be willing to put their own cash on the line. And a business champion is important in any community-based venture. Most people have other things going on in their lives, and, while they will support you, someone has to be the trail-blazer and be committed to keep on going."

Still, she continues, "Had any of us known the work involved, we likely would not have started. On the other hand, we had a dream, and it was important to go for it! None of us had any idea of the magnitude of local expertise within the community. This was the saving feature that ultimately made us financially viable. It did not matter what was required, someone locally had the expertise.

"In the end," she concludes, "you do what you have to do."

Marty Draude agrees with Colleen's approach. "Success must be clearly defined. This place is about achieving its goals. We have worked closely as a core group and written down our vision and goals. Colleen, of course, has given 150% since day one. She gave up her job to work on this venture full-time."

Marty himself trained as a chef and worked part-time to fill the staffing gaps. But for him, success is the journey, not the destination: "You must not be deterred. There will always be problems and reasons to quit. In fact, every day there is a good reason to quit, but we agreed, as a management team, to 'never say never'."

The project continued to grow as the core group identified the next levels. They had a three-phase vision of a house, a barn, and a church. The barn would include crafts and dances, and the church would be available for old-style country weddings. Of particular importance was the yard, which would be designed to give people an idea of the original beauty and attraction this land held for the thousands of people who homesteaded in Saskatchewan.

What kept them going, according to Marty, was "the fire in the belly. You must have it burning within you. In some ways logic is not necessary. You do what must be done, even if it appears impossible. That's the difference between a manager and a trail blazer, and it is the ultimate key to entrepreneurship."

At its height, Rose Bush Acres Heritage Resort Co-operative Ltd., to give it its full name, won the TISASK (Tourism Industry of Saskatchewan) Rookie of the Year Award in 1995, which provided the enterprise with an excellent profile during their first years. Constrained by a lack of funds for marketing and development, they relied heavily on word-of-mouth references and referrals. One of their biggest annual promotions was called *Harvest at the Manor*, usually held toward the end of September. The first year they expected several hundred people, but ended up with 4,500. It evolved into a two-day event with a full range of activities including cowboy poetry, trade shows, an artists' alley, crafts, and antique auctions.

"We had challenges in staffing, particularly in attracting and keeping qualified chefs," Colleen remembers. "Our initial concept was to recruit a live-in couple who would manage the business, and we built a suite in the basement for that purpose. A couple could make a very good living at this business, we thought. Up until late 1999 we were not able to find the ideal couple, but the opportunity finally came in December 1999 when the business was sold to Earl and Perla Werk, a couple from British Columbia who live on site and operate the business as a bed and breakfast establishment." After seven years, it seemed the time was ripe for Colleen and the other members of the management group to return to their other business activities. The dream of the Haussecker and the Draudes has been achieved according to their original vision.

10

Pound-Maker Agventures Ltd.

In the late 1960s the Saskatchewan agriculture landscape looked bleak. Grain markets were oversupplied, prices were low, and sales opportunities were few. Early in 1969, fifty Lanigan-area farmers decided to do something about it. Their survival, they knew, would depend on creating their own market.

The result of their efforts was Pound-Maker Agventures Ltd., which encompasses not only a 28,500-head cattle feedlot, but an ethanol plant that annually produces thirteen million litres of alcohol. The company employs fifty people, and buys three million bushels of barley and 1.5 million bushels of wheat every year.

"THE situation farmers face today is similar to 1970 when my father and others set the goal to supply an alternative market for grain through a commercial feedlot operation," according to Brad Wildeman, the president of Pound-Maker Agventures Ltd. and the son of W. A. (Bill) Wildeman, one of the company founders. "Farmers are desperate for alternatives. I guess the message is that alternatives are there, but communities have to be prepared to work together to make it happen."

The business got started in 1970 when grain prices and quotas were extremely low. The idea was to put the grain through cattle and hogs instead of the Canadian Wheat Board. Money was tight, but the original shareholders were creative. In the co-operative spirit, they each put up some cash to buy lumber for a few cattle pens, but they financed the feedlot primarily by contributing cattle, grain, and labour in exchange for shares in the company. The feedlot has expanded several times since 1973 and continues to thrive. It has grown in stages, starting at 4,000 head and expanding every three or four years. In 1990 there was a total

Pound-Maker Agventures Ltd., has 25,000 head of cattle in this feedlot near Lanigan, SK.

infrastructure upgrade, together with the ethanol plant, that increased the feedlot to 18,500. It was expanded in 1994 to 23,500, and again in 1998 to 28,500.

In September 1990, after exhaustive research and a number of feasibility studies, construction began on a 10,500-head feedlot expansion and a ten-million-litre-per-year ethanol plant. It was a ground-breaking enterprise for western Canada, and it demanded enormous energies from the Board of Directors. But it was a responsible, and ultimately profitable, decision.

Ethanol was seen as a means of diversifying the company and at the same time finding another way to use the grain. The co-products of the ethanol plant would be suitable for use in the feedlot. Wheat is the basis of ethanol production. With the addition of yeast and enzymes, the starch in the wheat is converted to ethanol and carbon dioxide. Co-products of the process, thin stillage and wet distiller's grain, are fully utilized in the feedlot. The thin stillage (in brewing alcohol, stillage is what remains of the mash after the distilling process) is fed to the cattle through the water distribution system, while the wet distiller's grain is mixed with barley, silage, and hay. The technology behind these wheat-based by-products is unique to Pound-Maker, and is the framework of the synergistic relationship that exists between the feedlot and the ethanol plant.

Today, Pound-Maker is an icon in the community, successful beyond the dreams of its founders. When that group first got together, they were sure of only two things: whatever they did, it would have to use large volumes of grain, and the venture must be community led. A feedlot seemed a natural choice. Each of the fifty became shareholders by committing $4,000 to the project: $2,000 in cash, and another $2,000 to be contributed in labour, at $1.75 per hour. The feedlot was built in 1970 and established as Pound-Maker Feeders Ltd. The name came not from the great Cree chief Poundmaker, but from the simple goal of "adding pounds" to cattle through the alternative marketing of grains. The first year was wildly successful. Approximately 4,000 head of cattle were brought in at 13¢ a pound. Grain at the time was only 25¢ to 30¢ a bushel.

The enterprise made a great deal of money that year, so the feedlot expanded, bringing in another 2,000 head the following year. By 1971, other communities in Saskatchewan were taking advantage of cheap grain to build similar operations. Then in 1973 beef markets collapsed. Grain prices rose dramatically, and community feedlots around the province were wiped out. Pound-Maker was crippled, but it didn't die. The community was committed to keeping the operation alive. Local shareholders frequently delivered grain on deferred payment to the feedlot, and Pound-Maker limped along until the markets recovered.

The experience was enough to show the shareholders that they needed a venture that would let them break free of agricultural cycles, something that would not be tied to beef or grain price fluctuations. They were adamant that the new undertaking be self-sufficient. No one wanted to be providing personal guarantees.

The shareholders heard about commercial and environmental potential of ethanol through a local entrepreneur, Eric Holle. Eric was something of a visionary. During the course of his career, he built a shopping centre in Lanigan, as well as a movie theatre, not to mention a 1,000-sow hog operation, a size virtually unheard of in the early 1980s. Eric was familiar with ethanol plants in Europe, and he provided the impetus the shareholders needed to proceed.

Pound-Maker had significant retained earnings to contribute toward the construction of the ethanol plant, but the bank was unwilling to put up the money unless Pound-Maker could produce a signed contract from a buyer. Mohawk Oil, the only company buying ethanol at the time, turned out to be very keen on Pound-Maker's integrated approach, with both a feedlot and an ethanol plant. They took a twenty-two percent share in the company and assisted in providing the expertise to build the plant.

The partnership with Mohawk was established toward the end of 1989. During the same period, it became obvious that the feedlot would need to expand to be competitive and to fully utilize the ethanol co-products. Once again, things fell into place. Through a strategic partnership with the Saskatchewan Wheat Pool, Pound-Maker moved from 8,500 head to 18,500 head in a single year.

With two strong corporate partners, the obligation from the local group for the construction of the ethanol plant was $750,000. They set themselves a target of $1.2 million—just in case. A private share offering was made, and the number of shareholders went from the original fifty to about 200. Local farmers and small business owners bought all the shares.

With such a huge enterprise on their hands, attention turned to ensuring that control of the venture would remain in the community's hands. Pound-Maker Feeders Ltd. was rolled into Pound-Maker Investments Ltd., so that community shares could be voted as one block. Pound-Maker Agventures Ltd. became the parent operating company. A Board of Directors was formed, with two seats held by Mohawk, two by the Saskatchewan Wheat Pool, and the remaining six allotted to Lanigan area shareholders. Community ownership of Pound-Maker represented fifty-six percent of total shares.

Further feedlot expansions took place in 1994 and again in 1998.

The original idea behind Pound-Maker, as with so many community ventures, was to create market opportunities for local farmers. It was an idea that remained close to the board's collective heart.

"The philosophy of Pound-Maker revolves around creating opportunities for shareholders, but not obligations," says Brad Wildeman. "We buy barley and wheat from our shareholders first. Next, we buy from the Saskatchewan Wheat Pool, then non-shareholders."

Pound-Maker has no need to own crop land and does not participate in grain farming. It pays a fair price for the grain it uses, and farmers receive payment on delivery. Pound-Maker also hauls manure to the crop land owned by shareholders, and in return for the manure, the shareholders supply straw bales to the feedlot, thereby benefiting the feedlot and enhancing the productivity of the land.

Pound-Maker offers a variety of delivery contracts for its shareholders, including basis and forward pricing opportunities. The company's open positions are covered on the Chicago Mercantile Exchange and the Winnipeg Commodity Exchange futures market as a means of managing the risk associated with forward pricing alternatives.

Not surprisingly, Pound-Maker has provided tremendous employment opportunities for the local community. The company, in fact, is the second largest employer in the Lanigan area, with approximately three-quarters of the fifty people who work there having been born and raised nearby. Some of them are also able to continue farming, thanks in no small part to the off-farm income Pound-Maker provides. About half the people at Pound-Maker are shareholders or the children of shareholders.

Pound-Maker is a strong foundation for the community. Young people have the opportunity to stay in the Lanigan area, simply because they don't have to leave home to get a job. The shareholders have always looked on the company's ability to sustain itself as being more important than any return on their investment. When Pound-Maker paid its last dividend in 1994, in fact, many shareholders felt it should have retained the earnings, to provide a shelter for tough times. Undoubtedly, the shareholders are committed to their community, the company, and the benefits it provides.

"People here think of Pound-Maker as their own," says Brad, "and take great pride in showing off the facilities to visitors."

Pound-Maker, in turn, is committed to buying locally and using local talent. "Many companies starting up today complain about not being able to find enough skilled labour," Brad notes. "There's a lot of talent around them, they just need to trust the people in their own areas."

The Pound-Maker operation is a superb example. The technology related to the utilization of ethanol by-products was developed by Pound-Maker people. "These people weren't engineers. They just had the opportunity to show themselves."

Pound-Maker is active in the community as well, sponsoring 4-H events and hockey tournaments, among other things. They try to be as involved as they can, to the point of paying a voluntary road-maintenance allowance to the community. As Brad says, "These people are who we are." Indeed, the company has grown and prospered largely through the creativity and hard work of its shareholders and employees.

Intensive livestock operations in Saskatchewan often come under close scrutiny, but Pound-Maker has not received a single formal complaint in all the years it has been operating. Individual farmers in the area, whether beef or grain, view Pound-Maker as an excellent local market, and the best part is that it is community owned. Most people view the odour as a small inconvenience compared to the benefits it brings to the community.

The success of Pound-Maker Agventures Ltd. has been owing largely to a committed and visionary Board of Directors and an extraordinary group of employees, shareholders, and farmers who have stayed with the business and supported each phase of its development. Its difficulties and challenges are those that face every business in Saskatchewan.

Mylles Wildeman, a distant cousin to Brad, grew up in the Lanigan area and farms 6,500 acres three miles south of Pound-Maker. Mylles also worked as a seventeen-year-old to build the original facility. He then studied commerce at the University of Saskatchewan, returning to Lanigan to farm in 1975. He has served on the board since 1985 and became very involved during the negotiations to bring in the ethanol plant. In 1990 he was appointed project chair of the ethanol plant for two and a half years.

"The most difficult part was putting the financing together," he recalls, "and bringing the Wheat Pool and Mohawk to the table. One very important lesson we learned is that you can't leave all the work to your consultants. Consultants can never replace the owners."

After negotiations stalled, Mylles was hired as the shareholder representative to negotiate directly with the joint-venture partners. He is careful to say, however, that he was only part of a much larger team: "A host of people have been involved in the company's success right from the beginning." His first love has always been farming, so after the ethanol plant was operational, he returned to it.

None of it, he points out, has been as easy as it might sound. There were times when the company faced severe financial challenges, but no one ever wanted to quit.

"Perhaps the next step is the direct retail of ethanol into the market, or packaged beef products through other synergistic business partners," says Mylles. "There is no question of standing still. We must keep innovating to stay profitable, and capitalize on new opportunities."

"Saskatchewan is a lot more competitive than we give ourselves credit for," Brad Wildeman adds. "We seem to have an inferiority complex. There is often the perception that we are not friendly to business. But we can do it here."

Pound-Maker is the proof.

11

Sandhills Essence

Hazlet sits on the edge of the Great Sand Hills in south-western Saskatchewan. It is known for farming, oil, the Hazlet Sandhills Players ... and soap. And not just any soap, but natural, healthy, old-fashioned soap made the old-fashioned way. This soap has really taken off in our modern society. And, like all popular ideas, it has grown.

The trio of Kathy Olsgard, Heather Ellis, and Janice Stock, who started a modest business they called Sandhills Essence in 1988, are perhaps a bit surprised by the scope of their success, but that hasn't prevented them from expanding their business to make bath salts, bath oils and gels, aromatherapy products, home spa products, and beeswax candles.

HEATHER ELLIS did not plan on becoming a businesswoman. All she wanted were some inexpensive Christmas gifts. "It was 1988," recalls the mother of four, who runs a farm with her husband near Hazlet. "We had a severe drought. There was no crop, and that meant no money." Heather suggested to her friend, Kathy Olsgard, that they team up to make some soap, which they would give away as Christmas gifts. The gifts were much appreciated by family and friends, who encouraged them to continue. Janice Stock joined the team shortly afterward. Within a few months they attended the Swift Current Fair, where they sold all their inventory. Sandhills Essence was on its way as a business enterprise.

Heather, Kathy, and Janice officially started their business in July 1990. They are part of a growing number of rural Canadian women entrepreneurs who, faced with the ever-rising cost of living, active young families, and job prospects near zero, have created home-based businesses.

"The idea came to us as a form of necessity," says Heather. "Our grandmothers used to make soap out of necessity, and so, in a way, it was passed along to us. We decided to revive an old tradition, but improve on the idea."

Many of today's commercial soaps are highly manufactured, and they've lost many of the unique characteristics and qualities of traditional soaps. Some commercial soaps aren't really soap at all, but chemical detergents. They are advertised as not leaving a soap film, but they tend to be caustic, and they dry out the skin.

"Despite my lifestyle of working with my hands and lots of outside living," says Heather, "my skin is moist and soft simply from using our soaps. The ingredients that provide the traditional cleansing action have a balance of natural oils that are beneficial and healthy for the skin."

Soap-making is not a terribly complex process, and the technologies involved are not new. People have been making soap for thousands of years. According to folklore, soap was discovered by ancient cleaners who were washing the altars on which burnt animal sacrifices had been offered. They found that the combination of rain water, animal fat, lye, and ashes resulted in a lather that was a very effective cleanser.

Kathy and Heather are farm wives who had little previous experience in starting a business, though Janice had operated a sewing manufacturing business since 1988. One thing they all had experience in was managing a farm, and that expertise helped them tremendously, particularly in terms of keeping an eye on costs and managing cash flow. It was the manufacturing and marketing aspects that presented a major challenge to the three women. "That took a lot of work and research by all of us," says Heather.

They started the business in the basement of Janice's house, because she had the most room. They had no business plan. They just kept track of costs and kept growing. Their current "factory" is an older two-storey house that was the original home on Janice's farmstead.

Since the three women live on farms that are quite isolated, it took some time to source the raw material. They spent a lot of time on the phone at the beginning. It was two or three years before they reached the point they are at now, and their isolation and the low surrounding population continue to be a problem. Transportation is both difficult and expensive, as there is no bus service to their town. In addition, they routinely lose sales because people prefer to shop in nearby Alberta to save the provincial sales tax.

Left to right: Kathy Olsgard, Heather Ellis and Janice Stock of Sandhills Essence in Hazlet, SK. Photo: Rosalee Hiebert.

Research and development are a major factor in their success. They did research on how to manufacture a range of moisturizing soaps and natural bath products, and studied the effects of different herbs, spices, and natural colouring agents. Their choices were based partly on the principles of aromatherapy, an ancient craft that uses traditional herbs and spices for a broad range of mental, spiritual, and physical treatments. Sandhills Essence now has an aromatherapist who works with the three entrepreneurs as a consultant on their formulations.

Janice, Kathy, and Heather are constantly developing new, complementary products. "We have a pretty good understanding of the basic science around making a soap that cleans as well as moisturizes," Heather explains. "We are currently working with hemp oil, which we produce on our farm. It is a very good moisturizer. We try all our new products on our family and ourselves, which is a pretty good sample."

The women also watch market trends, and they see a growing interest in natural products from organic foods and other more natural products. Their products are featured in gift shops and health stores, mainly in Saskatchewan, but the market is expanding. Over the years, they have seen a shift in their sales from farm families to a more urban market as the depressed farm economy has resulted in reduced net income. The cost of the products varies depending on input costs and labour, but some of their soaps can retail up to $3.50 a bar. They refuse to compromise on ingredients and quality simply to lower the price; they are in a quality niche market based on value.

Because all three partners live some distance from one another, they have arranged their schedule accordingly. Tuesdays are devoted to manufacturing. This has not changed since the beginning. "These are long days, but it fits in with our production schedules." says Heather. "Our processing requires some time for curing, and our recipes fit the weekly production cycle. We do everything on Tuesdays, including packaging and shipping orders. This has turned out to be the best way we can balance our other commitments to the farm and our families. We have focused on improving each production step and our output is now ten times what it was when we started."

"Some people have asked how three women can work together so closely for this long," says Janice. "We are three very different people." They do what is needed. Janice takes the calls and works in the office. Heather and Janice take care of ordering products. Kathy is the packaging expert. When problems arise, they get together and discuss possible solutions, then come to a consensus. In ten years of owning a business together, the three women have never fought. They do have differences of opinion, but they talk it through and work it out. Their working philosophy is based on having respect for one another and for each other's opinions.

"It is very challenging to separate business from long-term close friendships," says Heather. "But we all realize that business is business. This can be very hard, but we know it is the best for our business and for our friendship. We take the time to talk out all our issues and decisions, and this has been a clear formula for success."

They have never taken a loan for expenses. They never spend more than they have in the bank. When they are developing a new project they start small, since they must depend solely on sales for their capital. With growing families, they have had to share the tasks of marketing and attending trade shows. They each keep track of their time, and they are paid for what they do. The system has worked well for them.

Their community has been another major factor in their success. "People are proud of us," says Janice, "which makes us feel successful."

This success led to a feature article in the May 1997 issue of *Chatelaine* magazine. The women aren't sure how they were selected for the article, but it has had a tremendous impact on their business. "The *Chatelaine* article really gave sales a boost, particularly in the prairie region," says Heather. "We had new retailers and wholesalers approach us and old ones, who had dropped our line, called us for new orders." More important, however, was the feeling of pride that came with representing Saskatchewan rural business women.

"We were the first Saskatchewan company to produce soaps on this scale," says Heather. "Over the past few years there have been a number of competitors come on the market primarily due to our success. They want to duplicate our approach and make the same products. They call us for help and information, but we spent untold hours learning our business. We can't just give that away."

The partners recognize that Sandhills Essence has benefited from the increased number of companies selling special soaps, bath oils, shampoos, and fragrances. There has been a corresponding increase in market acceptance. On the other hand, increased competition means variable quality, and a consumer who has a bad experience with one company's product may not try others. This is unfortunate, as Janice, Kathy, and Heather are justifiably proud of their focus on innovation and quality.

"We have tended to be about five years ahead of the Saskatchewan market due to our research on consumer trends and new product development," says Heather. "The best example is the range of massage oils we developed over five years ago. Most stores wouldn't carry them. They thought it was too kinky. Today they are a common sight on store shelves."

As to the future, no one has asked to join the company, but neither have they looked to expand. But change is likely in the wind. They started ten years ago when all three of them had toddlers. The kids are now teenagers and have either left home or will leave in the next year or two. This will have an impact on the time available for the business.

Janice, Kathy, and Heather like the flexibility and independence of owning their own business. The only advice they have for others is be prepared to work long and hard. It is a gradual process.

To the outsider, it is perhaps easier to see that what really drives the company is the dynamic personalities of its three principals. Each has a unique set of skills. Their teamwork and synergy have worked well in the past, and have provided a strong foundation for the future, which looks bright.

Individual Ventures

12

Husband's Foods

Tucked onto the edge of the Moose Mountains in south-eastern Saskatchewan is a farm that will soon celebrate one hundred years of continuous farming by three generations of the same family. The bulk of the farm is comprised of 1,600 acres of prime land thirteen kilometers west of Wawota. The current generation does things a little differently than the previous two.

John and Carol Husband began their organic farming venture in 1989, converting from a purebred Polled Hereford livestock operation. The livestock business had been very good to them financially for over twenty years, but they needed to ease their work load. They decided to cut out the cattle operation and concentrate on the land.

SINCE 1967 the Husbands had marketed purebred Polled Hereford breeding stock directly to customers in Japan, Bulgaria, Czechoslovakia, England, and the United States, as well as throughout Canada. They knew many of their customers personally and understood what was important to them. They wanted to apply that kind of direct sales experience to grain marketing.

But after examining various conventional grain operations and speaking to farmers, they were dismayed. Grain farmers said they weren't making enough money, even though they were working longer hours and growing more bushels. Most of the time, they were completely shut out of the marketing process. The only way to increase profit was to increase acres, but that was invariably accompanied by an increase in the price of fertilizers and chemicals. Wheat and barley farmers, who have to sell to the Canadian Wheat Board, fared the worst. Not only were they hopelessly caught in the inputs squeeze, but to this day, in Carol's words, "they are legislatively forbidden from knowing anything about their business from the market point of view."

In conventional agriculture, it seemed, everyone but the farmer got a cut. Believers in the system continue to borrow money to grow grain to sell to unknown countries who many times have no money to pay, sometimes leaving the Canadian taxpayer stuck with the debt. To the Husbands, it did not seem like a profitable way to do business. While farm lobby groups continue to beg governments to solve their financial problems, the Husbands have grown to view governments as one of the chief problems.

"In the conventional grains industry," says Carol, "it became obvious to us that there were barriers between the farmer and the customer. This became one of the deciding factors for us to explore organic agriculture in greater detail."

"From a purely business point of view," John adds, "it appeared that there were some real opportunities in organic agriculture. The whole industry had been established with no government intervention, no subsidies, no central planning. In fact, the whole industry was consumer-driven, and still is. When you factored in the environmental aspects, growing consumer interest, and higher value markets, it made sense."

Their initial concern was what the neighbours would think. Organic farmers were considered off the wall in the 1980s. But John and Carol were already a bit out of the ordinary. Raised on farms but educated in the city, Carol was a teacher and John was studying mechanical engineering when his father died and he returned home to Wawota to manage the family farm. That was in 1966. It was not until the winter of 1988, after they had sold the pure-bred herd, that they began researching organic markets, and products such as flax and lentils and beans that appeared to be highest in consumer demand. Other producers endorsed what the Husbands had already guessed: that consumers were looking for quality organic food, and they were willing to pay a premium for it.

In their first summer of production, John grew thirty-eight varieties of beans in test plots, carefully monitoring their quality and extrapolating the yields to field scale. Carol, meanwhile, ran tests on the taste and cookability of the product. Focusing on consumer demand, the Husbands have gone in search of heritage varieties of cereals, oilseeds, pulses, and spices that had been bred over the generations mainly on the basis of taste. Conventional agricultural research tends to focus on yield, but the Husbands have found that their buyers are more interested in flavour.

The couple have restored a turn-of-the-century stone barn that had been built by John's grandfather. They use this as a market barn near Kenosee Lake during

86

A selection of the vegetables and herbs grown by Husband's Foods, Wawota, SK.

the prime summer months of July and August, selling a wide range of organic products from their own operation as well as unique items supplied by other farm families. On another farmstead, they have established a processing facility, with small cleaners, a gravity table, a drying building with racks for herbs and spices, and a storage shed for pallets. They have redesigned a house for bagging and processing. The company currently offers seven different soup mixes, each of which includes an easy-to-make recipe under the label. This marketing feature has paid off handsomely, with customers offering feedback about the soup mixes.

The market barn is open from 10:00 a.m. to 3:00 p.m. during July and August. Most of the customers are urban professionals, people who have travelled abroad or generally have an interest in a wide range of foods. Many drive quite a distance to buy specialty items and are eager to offer feedback on their previous purchases.

"They are very supportive," smiles Carol, "and make us feel good about what we do. The feedback—both encouragement and criticism—is priceless, both in terms of reflecting back to us a sense of value and pride in what we do, and in providing us with an opportunity to change and improve."

The Husbands' most surprising ally, they found, was the press. Whether in the local *Moosomin Spectator*, The Regina *LeaderPost*, or *Canadian Living* magazine, article after article has been both encouraging and kind. "Their generous support and genuine goodwill has brought many visitors who would ordinarily have never visited the farm," says Carol.

Although John and Carol market a portion of their huge range of cereals, oilseeds, pulse crops, and spices locally, the majority of their crops—cleaned, bagged, and shrink-wrapped—are sold in semi-loads throughout the year to the retail and wholesale trade.

Certified organic production requires strong management skills. The standards for certification are rigourous and demanding, and require detailed records of managing rotations and long-term soil fertility. Third-party inspectors ensure that industry standards for growing, storage, handling, and processing are met.

A key aspect of organic production and marketing is audit control, a system that enables anyone to trace a product backward through sales, handling, packaging, and harvest to the exact field on which it was grown, and the year in which it was grown. Growing numbers of consumers are willing to pay for this comprehensive "identity preserved" system. Issues such as mad cow disease, salmonella poisoning in poultry, bacteria in hamburger, and the debate over genetically modified food have heightened consumer awareness and concern about food safety and quality. With certified organic produce, they can be confident that the food they feed their families is guarded by a procedure that strictly prohibits pesticides and genetically modified products while at the same time helping to preserve the environment. Organic farmers, for their part, are convinced that the forces of nature cannot be manipulated on a sustainable basis; consequently, they attempt to produce their crops in an ethical partnership with nature.

Marketing is another important aspect of the organic farming philosophy. Every segment of the system, including the consumer, is considered an integral part of it. "Attempting to exert control over the consumer forces of the buying public is as futile as attempting to control nature," Carol maintains. The vibrant, diverse organic trade is rapidly becoming an alternative to the conventional food production and distribution system that has developed in North America. More and more consumers are reaping the benefits of it.

Organic farmers themselves are among the chief beneficiaries of organic production. Because they are not dependent on national and global commodity market forces, they are able to control the food production system through developing niche markets directly with customers. And they maintain a good profit margin at the same time.

The organic food industry has become one of the most lucrative markets in North America as more and more consumers seek organic grains, vegetables, fruits, and meats for health and environmental reasons. The most recent statistics (1997) indicate that there are over 750 certified organic farmers on the prairies, supplying food to a $5 billion market in North America that has been growing at an astounding rate of twenty-five percent per year.

Successful organic farmers are also successful marketers, as market information translates into dollars. With modern computer technology, market information can be accessed instantly from virtually anywhere in the world. Carol poses the question, "If you went to a top agency and asked them how to market Saskatchewan food products, what would they put in a campaign? Likely key visuals and words like delicious, wholesome, pure, healthy, certified, farmer controlled, safe, consumer sensitive, identity preserved. Well, you know, these are all elements of certified organic production." The philosophy of organic production is that it is farmer owned and farmer controlled; it is based on local markets first, then regional, provincial, national, and international. "Buy Local" is certainly not a new concept, but it works.

When the Husbands got started, they naturally asked experienced organic growers for advice. They quickly learned that organic farmers share agronomic information freely, and market information frequently. As a result, John learned a great deal very quickly, and that, together with his training as an engineer, helped him to build both a bean-picker and an herb-seeder, technologies that he shares with other growers.

The Husbands often get calls from discouraged farmers, usually producers with forty or fifty acres of broken grassland, who are hoping to capture a quick premium on the organic market. But there is no such thing as an instant organic farmer. Organic production is neither an easy nor a simple alternative. It takes financial resources to make the switch. Investments are required during the transition years when the farmer is learning alternative methods for pest control and soil fertility management. A range of equipment and proven techniques—including green manure crops, crop rotations, winter crops, inter-cropping and row-cropping—have resulted in effective weed control and the long-term maintenance of soil fertility for most organic farmers. But learning the techniques takes time, and buying the machinery takes money. There is also a great deal more work, including meticulous record keeping.

Carol Husband believes that the issue of what the neighbours will think is a big factor in holding many farmers back from practising organic agriculture. It goes against conventional wisdom. To many farmers, weeds in the field translate into poor farming practices. They have been taught for decades that weeds are bad—a concept that has been carefully nurtured by industry—and they must be controlled at any cost. All too often, that cost is the farmer's net profit.

Not surprisingly, many organic certifying bodies are experiencing a marked increase in interest from young farmers. Not only does it offer the hope of sustainable, healthy, and ethical production, it also seems to be one way that farmers can survive on the farm without off-farm income.

"Saskatchewan farmers have an enormous competitive advantage to benefit from this rapidly growing consumer-driven market," Carol believes. "This province is perceived as having pure water, clean air, and rich soils, along with cold winters that dramatically reduce the insects and disease that plague most other organic producers around the world."

Saskatchewan farmers have always focused on innovation, initiative, and wealth creation. If the producers and processors who make up the organic industry in Saskatchewan continue on the path of wealth generation and job creation within our communities, the organic food system will continue to put a great deal of money into the pockets of farmers. And nothing, so far, has ever proved better for the provincial economy.

13

Last Mountain Berry Farms Inc.

Barb and Barry Isaac were in the custom home construction business in southern California prior to moving to Southey, Saskatchewan in 1989 to start a new business. Barry had lived and worked in a number of locations in both Canada and the United States over the years. Barbara is an American citizen with landed immigrant status in Canada. She was disabled in an automobile accident in 1985, but fortunately there was no damage to brain function. At the time of their move, Barbara's children were adults, and she and Barry had recently married.

In their experience, "there are no significant barriers to doing business anywhere" in North America. "Saskatchewan became our location of choice for a number of business and personal reasons."

IT was Barb Isaac who saw the opportunity in processing and marketing saskatoon berries. During a visit to Barry's family homestead near Southey, she tasted his grandmother's saskatoon berry preserves. Her California market savvy and women's intuition got them thinking. "She instinctively knew that saskatoon berry preserves were unique and would sell if the quality and subtle taste could be maintained," says Barry, general manager of Last Mountain Berry Farms. They were recently married and looking for something different. "In mid-life, we moved to Saskatchewan and started over."

Barry's parents had both been raised on farms in the Southey area, but Barry spent much of his childhood in military communities across Canada as his father was in the service. During the war years, however, Barry and his mother lived in Southey with her parents.

"My maternal grandfather was a great influence on me," Barry recalls, "and those years as a young person on the farm had a lasting impact on me and my independent nature."

He liked being able to make decisions and then do what was required to get the job done, and he loved working with his hands. His grandfather encouraged his entrepreneurial spirit, with the result that Barry has been working for himself since he first set up as a cotton candy retailer at the Regina Exhibition. He was fourteen years old at the time.

Following his natural inclination to work with his hands, Barry began a twenty-year career as a home builder. He founded Star West Homes in Moose Jaw in 1975, building houses on speculation when the housing market was hot. When the Moose Jaw market softened in 1982, he moved to Vancouver, which had a booming economy and a shortage of housing. He established Oceanside Homes and again started building homes on speculation. A growing reputation soon brought him requests for custom building.

By 1985, he had become highly skilled in the construction of very large custom homes, a niche market that was expanding in the United States. When the Vancouver housing market softened, he re-located to Hermitt, California, near Palm Springs, and established Custom Homes by Barry. With a crew of four or five, the company built twelve to fifteen houses per year, ranging in size from 5,000 to 10,000 square feet.

It was in Hermitt that Barry met Barb, a native Californian with a background in health care. They married, and he brought her to Saskatchewan for Christmas in 1988 to visit his family. They stayed in his grandparent's farm home. Barry calls it serendipity.

"We actually made our decision quite quickly," he recalls. "The idea hit us during Christmas 1988. It took us a year to research the opportunity and wind down our construction business in California. We researched a range of native fruits in Saskatchewan, but ended up concentrating on saskatoon berries as the first major fruit for our business."

They settled on Barry's grandparents' homestead, and by June 1990 they had the first three acres of saskatoon berries in the ground. They had decided to take a step-by-step approach, first establishing a three-acre orchard to secure their supplies and then getting into processing in a year or two. But Mother Nature handed them an opportunity in the summer of 1991, providing an unusually large crop of wild saskatoon berries. Suddenly, the couple had

Barry and Barb Isaac of Last Mountain Berry Farms Inc., Southey, SK.

supplies beyond their business plan projections, so they decided to leap into production right away.

The farmstead had nothing suitable in the way of buildings. In fact, Barb and Barry started with a fruit storage and processing building that they also lived in. "We planned and built the 44' × 100' to get started, have a place to sleep, and space for future growth," the couple recalls. Ironically, it was a number of years before the professional house builders actually started on a house to live in—and it is still not complete. But they had a reason for building slowly. They had resources to invest in the new business, but they wanted to be totally self-financed and so they built what was required as the business could finance it. With good debt management, they minimized their financial risk and exposure. "Everything has gone back into the business to make it work," says Barbara.

The Isaacs decided that their focus would be on quality. Living in the heart of California fruit country, where her children grew up, Barb had been processing fruit in a small way all her life. "I was surprised by how much I already knew about the fruit processing industry," she says. She researched various fruit preservation processes and eventually decided on the more traditional methods, cooking and pasteurizing the fruit rather than using quicker and cheaper chemical preservatives. It was more labour intensive and costly, but it tended to enhance the quality of the end product. Their processing techniques certainly play a major role in the high quality and excellent taste of the product. "I've focused on the same high quality that I put into the jars for my family," she says: nutrition, safety, and no chemical preservatives.

Following the 1991 bumper crop, the Isaacs tried to use wild native stands as a continuing supply, but were always troubled by the inconsistent quality. Returning to orchard production, they soon developed good relationships with a network of saskatoon berry orchards in Alberta and later in Saskatchewan and Manitoba.

Again serendipitously, Southey is centrally located in the best saskatoon berry production area in western Canada, and Last Mountain Berry Farms is now the largest processor of saskatoon berries in Canada—probably in the world—with an annual requirement of almost 150,000 pounds. Although their own orchards are growing, they still have to buy 70,000 to 100,000 pounds of saskatoon berries annually to fill their orders.

Continuing to improve production, the Isaacs eventually reached the point where it became necessary to purchase a mechanical harvester. As the harvest season is often only two short weeks, it was critical that they have the capacity to take full advantage of it. Not surprisingly, no harvester had yet been designed for saskatoon berries, and the machine they bought required many modifications. Barry enjoyed the challenge. "Now it works quite well," he says modestly. Because the fruit does not ripen evenly, they have to harvest the orchard several times mechanically, but they still rely on hand picking to get the remainder of this valuable crop.

Barry's business acumen helped him identify market opportunities for native fruit. His experience in the custom home construction sector had taken him across North America, following the trends and the vibrant economies. His experience in large custom homes finely tuned his inclination to look for niche markets and to listen carefully to what the customers want. The Isaacs took a similar approach to identifying and developing a market for saskatoon berries.

"We tried to understand who was in the saskatoon berry market and where the trends were going," says Barry. "At the time, there was only one other major player, and that was the Riverbend Plantation in Saskatoon. They had established a strong position in the tourist and gift market. We decided to develop a parallel but non-competitive position in the general consumer market, which has worked very well for both of us."

In fact, Riverbend Plantation and Last Mountain Berry Farms have each grown steadily in size and success over the years, but without any direct competition. They stay in touch with one another, particularly in terms of securing supplies, and the relationship has been good for both the producers and the province.

Fortuitously, Last Mountain Berry Farms' intention to enter the commercial retail market coincided with the opening of Costco in Saskatoon and Regina. Costco became the company's first large retail customer, and was very supportive of locally produced foods, providing they were of high quality. Last Mountain Berry Farms was soon supplying all the Costco stores in western Canada. They now market to Costco/Price Club, Superstore, and to the Ontario-based ELCO Fine Foods, Canada's second largest distributor of food products.

"Our own success," according to Barry, "is related to the fact that saskatoon berries are a novelty, unique, and in some ways rare. We currently market to a provincial and regional market where consumers know the fruit and it sells well. It will be another challenge when the domestic market is saturated and we must look at marketing outside the traditional areas, to Ontario and into the United States."

Over the years the Isaacs' orchards have expanded steadily, to the point where they now have fifteen acres, irrigated by a trickle system using a dugout as the water source. "Access to water and good pest control management is the key to a good quality crop every year that secures our base supply," says Barry.

The Isaacs are now looking at other fruit products to augment their saskatoon berries production. "Once you have the equipment and markets, it makes sense to expand to other fruits," says Barry. They use the available supplies of wild black cherries (the market name for chokecherries) for syrups, and they also import blueberries, blackberries, raspberries, and strawberries, mostly from British Columbia. The fruit arrives in frozen form, is processed, then shipped back to Vancouver for the consumer market. This is precisely the reverse of what happens with the majority of Saskatchewan's agricultural products, but, as Barry asks, "Why not do more value-adding right here in the province?"

Barry and Barb are naturally supportive of the continued development of Saskatchewan's fruit industry. It may never be really large, but Barry believes there are significant improvements that could expand the industry in the province. As fruit production increases, for example, there is a real need for someone to manage the collection, storage, and distribution of the raw product to the processors. Many orchards are coming into the market from across the province. A coordinated supply of product to the processors is needed to manage and maintain quality.

Barry and Barb have made a significant impact on fruit producers and processors in the province, not least by demonstrating that a fruit processing venture can be successful in a small village. With eight full-time and twenty-five part-time employees, Last Mountain Berry Farms Inc. makes a significant contribution to the local economy.

When asked about the key to their success, Barry replies, "Take one step at a time, believe in your product, and know what you are doing. You must also be persistent with your marketing and consistent in your presentation. You must show confidence in yourself and your product. But our personal definition of success is to do something because you enjoy it," says Barry.

The Isaacs derive a great deal of satisfaction from the fact that people are happy with their product. "We aim to provide a quality product at a reasonable price. We do not want to be the biggest, but we do want to be the best."

14

Drake Meat Processors Inc.

Kelly Ediger has a strain of entrepreneurial blood in his veins that goes back many generations. In 1958, his father, Norm Ediger, left dairy farming to manage a co-operative locker plant in Drake, Saskatchewan. He exercised an option to buy in 1960 and operated the business as Drake Locker Plant Ltd., a custom slaughter, processing, and storage facility. He also made custom sausages for the local market.

After running the business for twenty two years, he sold it to his son in 1980. In 1981, Drake Locker Plant burned to the ground. "There is nothing like a fire to focus your attention on the future," Kelly reflects. "I had to decide what to do next."

KELLY EDIGER grew up helping his father in the locker plant. They both loved the meat business, and each liked idea of being his own boss. As Kelly remembers, "My father had an impact on me from a number of points of view. Working with him as I grew up developed my love for hard work and for being in control of my own business."

Norm also understood Kelly from the point of view of a young man full of ideas. He gave Kelly the freedom to travel and go to school. As a result, the younger Ediger visited Europe and the Caribbean, and has travelled throughout the United States. He attended high school at Rosthern Junior College, studied at a Bible School in Swift Current for two years, and spent a further two years at Fresno Pacific College, majoring in Theology and Biblical Studies. From there he went to Taylor University in Upland, Indiana.

After thoroughly exploring his vast range of other interests, Kelly returned to Drake to enter the meat business with his father. An inter-generation business transfer is not always an easy process, and Kelly was grateful to his father for "giving me the chance to spread my wings, to try other things. I came back on my own terms."

When Norm sold the business to Kelly in 1980, he literally turned it over and let him get on with it. "I made mistakes," Kelly reflects, "but they were necessary in order to get my feet under me as a business owner and manager. Dad still remains an integral part of the business, and I rely on him a great deal."

After the devastating fire, and with his father's support, Kelly decided to build a new plant. They were open for business a year and a half later, which was longer than Kelly had expected. As he was learning, there are lots of government hoops to jump through when you're building a meat processing facility. But there was help from the government, too. It was a grant from the Department of Regional Economic Expansion, covering about one-quarter of the capital cost of the new building, that helped make possible the decision to rebuild.

"We might not have gone ahead without this grant support," says Kelly. "It really helped."

Before the fire, the plant had a handful of employees and did custom slaughter and packaging for local farmers and hunters. But times were changing. By 1980 there were fewer livestock producers in the region, and people tended to purchase their meats as needed. The demand for carcasses was declining.

When the doors of the new business opened, the company continued as a custom processor, but Kelly saw that it would be necessary to diversify if he was going to survive. Having formulated several popular sausage recipes in the past, he decided to try manufacturing specialty meat products for wholesale through neighbouring grocery stores. It soon became apparent that the demand for Drake Meat products would sustain further market development.

Kelly expanded the local market to the surrounding communities of Watrous, Lanigan, Wynyard, and Strasbourg. He then hired a manager to direct a more aggressive marketing program. In 1986, with eight employees, the company began to expand its focus to the rest of Saskatchewan. New people were hired for the increased demands of accounting, sales, production, packaging, and distribution. By 1999 the company employed close to sixty people, and the market was still growing.

The first major retail chain to carry Drake Meat products was Western Grocers. They were followed by Federated Co-operatives, Safeway, IGA/Codville, and finally Price Club/Costco. Clearly, hiring a full-time director of marketing was a key factor in the rapid development of market access to the mainline grocery chains. Drake

Volker Otto, an employee, removes a rack of sausage at Drake Meat Processors Inc., Drake SK.

Meat products are now available throughout Saskatchewan under the Homestead Cabin label. The product lines have expanded from a few sausage recipes to fresh-packed sandwiches, beef jerky, a full line of sausages, smoked hams, marinated kabobs, side ribs, tenderloins, and a variety of beef, pork, and bison burgers. Relying on their own distribution system, four trucks weekly deliver some 200 product types to independent stores across the province.

Dave White, the marketing manager at the time, believes that a large part of the company's rapid growth was attributable to one principle: never ignore the customer. "We spent a great deal of time with demos in stores and trade shows and listening to what our customers said about our products and the new recipes and innovations we tried," he says. "Our focus was the Drake Meat farmer sausage market. We developed unique packaging and flavours and, through demos, created our own niche market throughout Saskatchewan. We are in all retail stores across Saskatchewan simply because the customers demanded to have Drake Meat farmer sausage in their local stores."

Drake Meat are currently licensed only for provincial distribution. In order to sell outside the province, they would have to be a federally inspected facility, a process both complex and costly, given the small processing volumes. Drake Meat has thus developed a successful market on the population base of one million people—a remarkable accomplishment by any measure.

They have rounded out their market with prepared, vacuum-packed sandwiches for independent retail gas stations in Saskatchewan. This supplementary market has allowed Drake Meat to hire a night shift to keep the facilities working twenty hours a day. The delivery trucks bring in raw materials and processing supplies as back-haul.

Research and development have been the key factor in finding a market niche for the company's products. Even though Kelly is the president, he spends the majority of his time on the processing floor because he is also responsible for directing the research and development. In this context, the company has received important research support from the University of Saskatchewan, and the Food Innovation Program in particular.

"Dan Prefontaine was in charge of the meat development program," Kelly explains, "and provided us with excellent support as we experimented with innovative techniques in meat processing. The biggest help was in improving the food safety and quality control aspects of our production process."

Kelly believes that this is the best way for government to support business development in the meat-processing field. The university has state-of-the-art labs and processing facilities for teaching and to support industry development. Another benefit of having meat processing experts at the university was that they could help Drake Meat secure equipment for the new products they were developing. "They were particularly helpful in helping us locate good quality used equipment," says Kelly, "which is important for cost control in small businesses."

In the fall of 1997 Kelly took in a partner and minority shareholder, his long-time friend Peter Nicholson. Peter, also an alumnus of Rosthern Junior College, had owned the local Shop Rite—later Shop Easy—for years before selling it. Kelly and Peter had been joint-venture partners in other businesses over the years and have a proven record of working well together.

"I was looking for someone to share the burden of a growing company," Kelly explains. "Our planned expansion required capital, and Peter's equity injection made a major difference on our balance sheet."

Kelly characterizes both Peter and himself as "easy going, but we complement each other's skill sets very well. We hire the type-A personalities that we need for the business and then manage their energies and innovation."

They had not done much in terms of formal business planning until 1995, but now they spend more time thinking and planning for the future. Knowing they could never compete in the high-volume, low-price markets, they have always aimed at the medium- to high-quality markets with premium pricing. This has turned out to be the best fit for the company. They compete for a smaller upper-end market that suits their production capacity.

As they expanded, Kelly was drawn more and more into the day-to-day management of the company. "I did not particularly enjoy this aspect of the company," he admits, "and I was not particularly good at it, either." It was this realization that led him to hire professional managers and human resource staff, allowing him to return to his major area of interest and expertise, which was research and product development on the processing floor.

The experience of the fluctuating hog and beef markets in the past years has given Drake Meat insights into the advantages of vertical integration, from the slaughter facility to the wholesaler. It was initially perceived as an advantage for maintaining the quality of their products, but they have also been able to manage their margins better as the company gets most of its hogs and beef from local farmers.

The key to success for Drake Meat Processors has been in learning how to make the most of their opportunities even when they presented themselves in the form of problems. The Edigers did it by developing a local niche market based on customer demand and then building brand loyalty. Once in charge of the company, Kelly learned how to delegate senior management tasks in order to maximize his natural skills and interests in product development. Last, he effectively used expanded partnerships to build equity, share the work load, and to plan the continued expansion of the business.

15

Riese's Canadian Lake Wild Rice

In today's world you can do anything you want from anywhere you want. By choice, we live and operate an international marketing company from a beautiful but remote bay twenty-five kilometers north of La Ronge. Overnight courier may take three days to reach us, but telecommunication technology gives us instant access to our customers in Europe and Asia. Doing business from La Ronge is not much different from other, more practical locations. It takes an ability to think big, have a positive attitude, and build a good network.

— K. Lynn Riese

IN 1998 Riese's Canadian Lake Wild Rice harvested a record 420,000 pounds from 1,400 seeded acres and purchased another 800,000 pounds of green wild rice locally to supply a network of markets around the world. It was an excellent year. But, like their southern counterparts, wild rice growers can quickly see their profits turn to losses because of bad weather or poor markets. The summer of 1999 brought unusual weather and high water levels, reducing production to 200,000 pounds. But Lynn Riese still expected to buy an additional 600,000 pounds to boost his inventory and meet the requirements of his market.

Wild rice—which is not really rice at all, but a type of grain—is planted in the fall, but will reseed itself if enough nutrients are available. It has quirky growing habits, though. Some years it is difficult to tell where it will grow, or if it will grow at all. In one planting season, Lynn seeded fourteen new bodies of water in an effort to boost production. Only one produced any positive results.

During the harvest season, from late August until the first killing frost, the naturally green wild rice is harvested from the lakes and shipped to either of two processing plants in the province. There the product is roasted and dehydrated, reducing its weight by half. Of this processed crop, only about forty percent will pass Riese's quality standards and capture premium prices.

Harvest season is hectic, and never takes less than six weeks. Harvesting starts at sunrise and continues until after dark. Airboats skim the water at fifteen to twenty km/hour, a front scoop harvesting the wild rice into a screen on the back. The grain ripens unevenly, and harvesters must revisit the growing areas up to six times each harvest period.

Facing almost certain uncertainty, Lynn Riese has worked hard to overcome the vagaries of the weather and the markets. The largest independent wild rice grower in Saskatchewan, he has led the Canadian industry in elevating his crop to the status of a specialty product that commands a premium. He has added value through focusing on quality, understanding the marketplace, and accommodating consumer trends. And he has protected his operation by developing an export market for a premium product aimed at European and Asian specialty markets.

Lynn Riese is no stranger to business development in northern Saskatchewan. Without much formal training, he has succeeded in a number of challenging areas. He grew up in La Ronge, in a society that saw little value in formal education, and quit school as a teenager to enter the work force. He decided on a career in flying, and trained in Prince Albert, Saskatoon, and Winnipeg. He became a successful commercial bush pilot. Working in northern Canada, he advanced as far as he could in the aviation industry by the time he was thirty years old. He aspired to something more, so he decided to return to La Ronge and go into business for himself.

Opening two restaurants in two years was not enough to satisfy his aspirations, so he decided to grow wild rice. He took some of the family capital and embarked on a voyage of exploration. Wild rice grows in bays and shallow water with lots of sunlight. The clearer the water, the better. With these criteria in mind, Lynn and his son, Kirk, found Meeyomoot Lake, which had one of the best bays of the fourteen northern lakes they explored. They leased the growing area from the provincial government. They planted wild rice and it grew. By 1983 they had made their first sale, so they planted more. But there were scores of other northern wild rice growers in the province, and many more in Manitoba and Ontario. In 1984 supply exceeded demand, and the crop cost more to produce than the growers earned. Undaunted, Lynn added a marketing/wholesaling arm to his operation.

He had always intended to create a marketing company that would sell not only his harvest but that of his fellow growers. By doing so, he would be providing a much-needed local service, and he would have a larger amount of product to market. He considered it an advantage that the product he was marketing was totally unlike the domesticated strains of wild rice grown in paddy fields in Minnesota and California: "Our rice is produced in the northern lakes and is considerably different in taste and texture."

By 1985 he had sold his restaurants and was marketing his own and other growers' wild rice to wholesalers, restaurants, and stores. He didn't have much experience in marketing, but, typically, he threw himself into the task of learning and doing at the same time. Initially, he placed ads in various publications such as *Canadian Geographic* and *Beaver Magazine*. He later travelled south to market his product directly to restaurants such as Cousin Nik's in Saskatoon and the Diplomat and the Sheraton in Regina. This worked well, but not well enough to turn a profit.

He tried the value-added route in an attempt to increase consumption and awareness of his product. The Rieses produced wild rice flour, wild rice pancake mix, and popped wild rice snacks. Unfortunately, the low recognition factor of wild rice itself made these value-added products even more difficult to sell. What they were doing, in fact, was processing a high-value primary product into a low-value, "value-added" product. "It simply did not make any sense to try and add value through processing," Lynn concluded. "We were clearly much better off adding value through niche marketing as a premium product to specialized customers."

Lynn travelled further afield, attending trade shows and food fairs throughout Canada, the United States, and eventually Europe. He was often accompanied by his wife Iris and their eldest daughter, Raelyn.

Although wild rice is the only wild grain native to North America, ninety percent of North Americans either don't know what it is or have never tasted it. Since the majority of buyers were unfamiliar with this northern delicacy, the Rieses always distributed wild rice recipe books at their booth. It was a clever marketing tool, and it helped to create a unique identity for the crop. Still, most retailers focused on the bottom line, and Riese's premium-priced wild rice could not compete with the lower-priced paddy-grown variety.

It took several years for Lynn to identify the problem: the target audience was wrong. The market most interested in wild rice dishes, he discovered, was considerably more upscale than he had anticipated. While traditional rice-eating areas such as Japan and India were difficult markets to break into because the

K. Lynn Riese, of Riese's Canadian Lake Wild Rice, La Ronge, SK.

product was seen as competition for local growers, or the dark colour of the product was not appealing, Europeans were immediately attracted by its quality, nutrition, and taste. Since the Europeans discovered wild rice, in fact, production in Saskatchewan has increased by more than four thousand percent. Still, it wasn't until 1988 that Lynn made a profit.

Thanks to his aggressive marketing, others have benefited from this growing industry over the past twelve years. In 1992, Riese's Canadian Lake Wild Rice and thirteen other recipients were honoured with Canadian Export Awards for excellence in exporting products and services around the world. This prestigious national award is based primarily on percentage increases in annual sales.

Riese's Canadian Lake Wild Rice currently represents twenty-one percent of all Canada's wild rice exports, and eight percent of global exports. In 1998, he turned over $1.5 million in annual sales. He buys most of his product from ninety northern growers, many of them First Nations, and employs eight full-time and twenty part-time staff himself.

His workday is likely to start at any hour out of the twenty-four. His European customers call during their business hours, not his. He keeps an office phone by his bed, and cheerfully answers it "any time of day, seven days a week." It's all part of his service. His customers—particularly those from Europe, who demand a top-of-the-line product—keep coming back because of the quality of the rice, and the high level of service his company provides.

"You must work within the entire marketing system," Lynn advises. "Everyone has to make money, from the producer on the lakes to the European retailer. You can't just dump the wild rice and expect it to sell."

In 1997, Lynn won a trip to Australia from Canadian Airlines Foundation's small business expansion program. "We try to set up distribution in different countries," he explains, "and try to do at least a country a year." His products are currently available in every European nation, the United States, and some Pacific Rim countries.

Versatility is the operative word in regard to marketing wild rice. "The Canadian industry is not without its problems," he says. "We have our own internal issues and continue to struggle with competing U.S. paddy wild rice, which is sold at a much lower price." And there are still only a few marketers in the Canadian industry, which is indicative of the high risks and sometimes low margins that characterize the business. But the very fact of Lynn Riese's survival in the business for over seventeen years, and his growing customer base, indicates that there is a solid place in the world for Canadian Lake Wild Rice.

In purely practical terms, Lynn's job involves making long-term arrangements with distributors, keeping track of orders, overseeing product shipments from their warehouses in La Ronge and Saskatoon, and keeping in constant contact with customers. He spends hours on the phone each day, and days away from home every year.

On a more philosophical level, being successful in international enterprise requires a good understanding of people and their cultures. Lynn's European customers, for example, demand the highest quality and believe, "There's no such thing as an excuse." They demand precision. It also requires motivation, self-confidence, initiative, and the ability to analyze different markets.

"Market and business planning were major factors in our success," says Lynn. "We really jumped ahead when my daughter, Raelyn, joined us, with her background training in marketing. We became much more focused on our market, and much more strategic in the use of our resources."

Although Lynn has clearly made a success of his business, he thinks the road would have been less bumpy if he had had a stronger educational background. "If I were to do it over again," he says, "I would have taken marketing and bookkeeping. I had to learn through the school of hard knocks, and that's always more expensive." A strong advocate of education, he is proud of his three daughters, who have all done well at university. He continues to sign up for business courses whenever he can.

"Establishing a market for your product is like making a snowman," he reflects. "Once it is built, you must keep working on it every day, even if you just want it to stay the same size."

Competitors come and go. As an industry leader, Lynn has noticed that they tend to go after his customers and markets most aggressively every time he has a good year. Invoking another analogy, Lynn compares wild rice marketing to trench warfare. His competitors usually have deeper pockets and more resources than he does. Rather than meet their attacks head-on, the Rieses hunker down in the trenches, thus avoiding direct hits and crippling bursts of corporate shrapnel. Inevitably, the enemy runs out of ammunition. The Rieses get out, dust themselves off, assess the damages, and go at it again. "The best defence is a good relationship with your customers," says Lynn. "Be persistent, consistent, watch your budget, and you will be a survivor."

The Rieses face essentially the same challenges as southern farmers in trying to market a primary commodity. Because of their unique crop, however, they took the initiative to focus on quality and enter the gourmet specialty markets, aiming at specific customers. They soon realized how important it was to know their customers on a personal basis. This necessitates a number of trips to Europe each year, as well as issuing invitations to visit their operation in La Ronge. The result has been a successful family business operation, the satisfaction of creating something new for a customer, and, perhaps most important to Lynn Riese, making a significant contribution to the economic development of the local economy.

16

Banach Winery

More than once we went to bed exhausted, thinking we would quit. It was such hard work and everything was moving so slowly. But each morning we seemed to have renewed energy to keep on going.

— **Diane Banach**

DIANE and Walter Banach had an uphill battle getting their Saskatchewan winery operational. Much of what they wanted to do had never been done before. They even had to get provincial legislation changed in order to sell their product. It took a long time and hundreds of letters, forms, and telephone calls. But in the end their perseverance paid off. The support and encouragement of the community, including their local MLA, helped keep them going.

The key to their success was focus: the Banachs never lost sight of what they wanted to do. Diane, a schoolteacher for many years, had always thrown her spare-time energies into producing a range of fruit wines. She took her hobby very seriously, and over sixteen years she had developed her own unique recipes and techniques. Turning her hobby into a commercial venture seemed a natural next step. But developing a commercial wine with commercial equipment was a different proposition than producing small batches at home. In the early stages, the Banachs visited some of Canada's best wineries in the Niagara peninsula and in British Columbia, and were fortunate to meet a couple of experienced fruit vintners who offered them valuable advice and assistance. As it turned out, though, actually making the wine was the simple part.

Their biggest problem was getting permits to allow them to sell their wine privately, a practice that is restricted under the Liquor and Gaming Act. Government regulations stipulate that alcoholic products must be sold in provincial Liquor Board Stores. To sell directly from their winery, the Banachs had to get a special permit, and to get the permit they had to submit a detailed business plan.

"We had not anticipated the roadblocks," says Walter. "We didn't know the bureaucracy. On the other hand, we did get some great support and assistance from people at the Liquor and Gaming Commission."

Once the permit was granted—after a year and a half—they began making their fruit wines. They offer four different types. Battle River Red is made primarily from chokecherries, which they market as "wild black cherries." Harvest Gold is made from crab apples, and is the only crab apple wine on the Canadian market. Lady Di, a blush wine, is made with strawberries, and Sir Walter is a raspberry wine.

"Our wines are made from the pure juice of the fruit," says Diane. "There are no additives or flavourings. Other fruit wines are generally made from an apple juice base, and then flavoured."

Establishing Banach Winery in a prime location in Battleford, at the corner of the main street intersections, has certainly helped the two entrepreneurs in terms of a visual presence. "We get regular tourist traffic during the summer," says Walter. "Visitors can tour the winery, and most will buy a few bottles."

Most of their product, however, is sold through provincial liquor stores. They produce enough wine to be stocked in most of the major outlets across the province, but, as Walter says, "We do not have the volumes to be everywhere."

"We are now able to move product into Alberta," Diane adds, "which has different regulations regarding the marketing of wines."

Depending on how well they do in Alberta, the Banachs will consider Manitoba as the next step, and perhaps the United States.

In Saskatchewan, the retail price of the wines is set by the Liquor and Gaming Act, based partly on the cost of production but also according to various taxes, bottle deposits, and mark-ups. The Banachs receive a relatively small return from the total price and feel that the government receives a great deal more.

"It is an on-going negotiating process with the government," says Walter. "We keep hoping for some changes that will allow us to do more direct selling of our products. It would be good for our business, good for customers, and good for the economy."

Diane and Walter's investment and operating capital comes entirely from the profit on sales. They don't have the resources for additional staffing, so the two of them do what they can and rely on part-time help during bottling. "The business

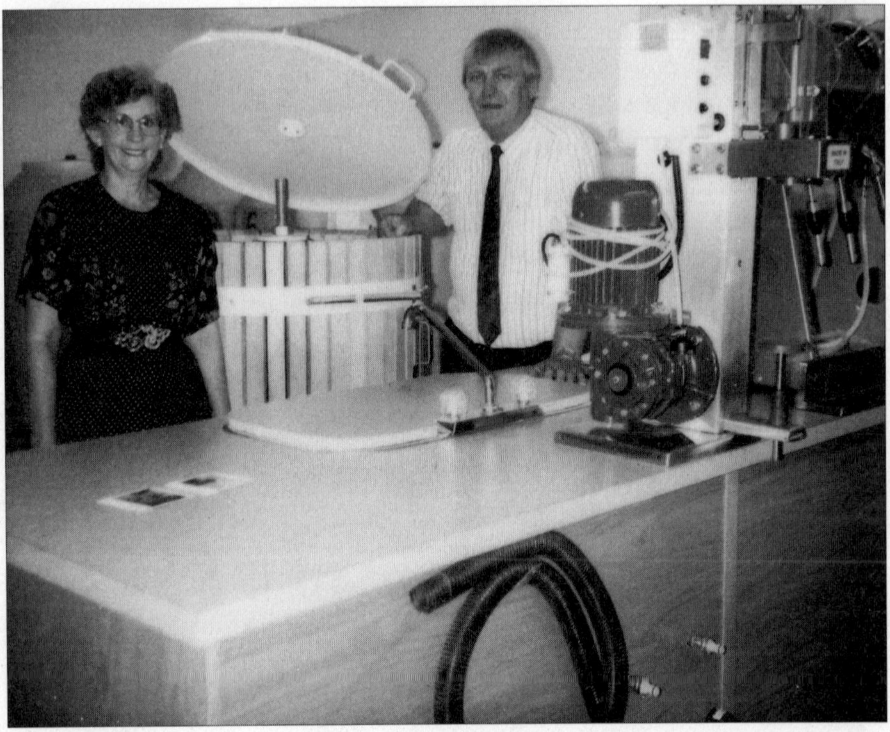

Diane and Walter Banach of Banach Winery, Battleford, SK.

could expand much more quickly without the restrictions on pricing and marketing," Walter points out.

Banach Winery has received some funding support through the Partnership Agreement on Rural Development (PARD) that has helped them with initial market development costs, while the Partnership Agreement on Water-Based Economic Development (PAWBED) helped with building renovations as the company grew. PARD and PAWBED are both federal-provincial cost-shared programs designed to encourage economic development activities in rural Saskatchewan. Both programs are administered by the Prairie Farm Rehabilitation Administration (PFRA), Saskatchewan Economic Development, and the Saskatchewan Water Corporation. (Around 1997 PAWBED and PARD were phased out, but PARD was replaced by CARDS [Canadian Adaptation and Rural Development in Saskatchewan].)

Diane and Walter are justifiably proud of the point they have reached with their business in five short years. "It's definitely not a business you become rich in," Diane admits, "but we have certainly learned a lot, met a number of great people, and feel proud of our accomplishments."

All marketing for Banach Winery is done by Diane or Walter, and they are pleased with the media interest in their business. Aside from launching their own modest advertising program, which includes the odd television commercial and newspaper advertisement, they have been interviewed on television and radio, and business reporters have featured the winery in newspaper stories.

Diane handles the bulk of the administrative work, and has competently taken charge of public relations, handling questions and comments from the public and the media alike. Walter manages the shop floor, dealing with production on a day-to-day basis. Major decisions are always made together. "We never make a decision without consulting the other first," says Diane. "If there are problems or a difference of opinion, we discuss it, let it sit for a while, or come to some kind of compromise."

Although Banach Winery is the only operation of its kind in Saskatchewan, Diane and Walter are continually fielding calls from people all over Saskatchewan wanting advice and information on how to get started in a fruit winery. As Walter points out, however, "We have worked extremely hard to learn the industry and to carve a market niche for our products. We'll offer anyone a tour of our winery, and then wish them the best of luck and tell them it is best to experience everything themselves."

"Starting up, for us," Diane adds, "was very difficult, because there were so many unforeseen expenses." But despite the challenges of working with government and a complex and seemingly overwhelming tax structure, the business continues to succeed. Still, the Banachs describe their profit situation as "marginal," largely because of the red tape and the bureaucratic road blocks they keep running up against.

"Turning a hobby into a business can be a good idea," Diane advises. "It allows you to bring a great deal of knowledge into a new venture, but still, it doesn't guarantee that you will make money. We would recommend to all entrepreneurs that they have some kind of financial backing during the start-up years. This is essential because expenses have a way of growing beyond expectations."

Diane suggests that the government could do more in Saskatchewan to help small businesses. The regulations and taxes are binding, confusing, and largely unnecessary. Government should be a help to small business, not its major problem.

The Banachs receive a lot of encouragement to "keep on keeping on" from themselves and their relationship. Diane also likes meeting with customers and doing samplings for groups or individuals. "The greatest reward is seeing your customers enjoying the product," she says. "You cannot buy that kind of satisfaction."

Her advice to new entrepreneurs is to research your business thoroughly, get help in forecasting expenses so you aren't surprised later, and finally, start gradually. Don't rush anything.

"In some ways," Diane reflects, "the business has taken longer to establish than we expected, but other parts of the business have progressed better than we anticipated." They are pleased that they are able to supply most Saskatchewan liquor outlets, and excited at the opportunities presented by their expansion into Alberta. And they have stayed focused: "We are always planning for the next expansion of our facilities, and new types of wine."

17

Rugged Country Manufacturing

Bob Cockwill has always had a knack for business. It started in grade two, when he organized his classmates to collect bottles for him, which he then recycled for profit. This entrepreneurial spirit came into play again when the Birch Hills resident and his wife Heather founded B&H Canvas—now know as Rugged Country—in 1992 to manufacture sports bags. Bob is an electrical contractor by profession. He and Heather had no previous experience in the apparel or textile business, but they did not let that deter them from pursuing a dream.

BOB COCKWILL grew up in a number of rural communities in Saskatchewan. His father's job with the Department of Natural Resources took the family variously to Hudson Bay, Carrot River, and then Buffalo Narrows. It was in Meadow Lake that Bob finished high school and took his first job, working in a hardware store, then a car dealership business where, over two years, he learned some of his selling skills. His love for sports took him to his next job, another prairie hybrid that incorporated a service station, motel, and sporting goods business under the same banner. Bob was soon managing the front end of the business, including the sporting goods section, and he stayed there for three years.

He then moved to Hudson Bay to work with MacMillan Bloedel for five years as an electrical apprentice, then journeyman. His next career step was to Melfort, where he joined 44 Trail Electric. Nine years later, in 1982, he moved to Birch Hills to set up his own electrical contracting company, Flyer Electric Ltd.

A sports lover as well as an aggressive marketer, Bob wanted to support the local teams. His idea was to provide sports bags with the name "Flyer Electric" printed on them. When he found that the only sports bags he could buy were

Left to right: Phillip Marzo, Robert and Heather Cockwill, Janice MacKinnon (Minister of Economic and Co-operative Development), Jack Langford (MLA), and Wayne Boyle (Mayor), cutting the ribbon during the grand opening of Country Leathers, March 1, 1999, in Birch Hills, SK.

made outside Canada and were of very poor quality, he decided to take matters into his own hands.

"That's how we got into the business," he laughs. "We started trying to make a much better quality sports bag that could carry our company name with pride."

He and Heather decided that there was a market to capitalize on. But identifying a market niche and succeeding in business don't always go hand in hand. "There was a lot of door-to-door selling in the early days," Bob remembers. "We wore ourselves out, but we saw a return from our hard work and it kept us going."

Bob and Heather were well aware of the risks of starting up a new venture in rural Saskatchewan, but they were confident that their goal of replacing poor-quality imported sports bags with a better-quality domestic version was a sound business idea.

It would have been understandable if they had questioned their decision in the early months, as they spent hours ripping apart and re-sewing items to meet the rigid requirements they had established. But the Cockwills knew that producing a top-quality product was essential if they were to be competitive, so it was a hardship they accepted. It was from that early experience that the company motto emerged: "We make it better, we make it yours."

The name of the company evolved from B&H Canvas to the more descriptive Rugged Country, and the range of products evolved with it. Rugged Country now offers some 200 items, ranging from leather jackets and sports bags to wheelchair supports and auger tubes. Twenty Rugged Country employees turn out the products at their facility in Birch Hills.

The customer base has also expanded into the west, as far east as Prince Edward Island, into the United States, and even down under to Australia. In a spectacular accomplishment for a firm that started out with three employees, the company won the contract to be the exclusive supplier to the Air Canada Cup Midget Hockey Tournament in Prince Albert in 1999.

"It does get easier as you get established," says Bob. "But we still had to hustle to win the Air Canada contract."

Marketing is always a challenge, but Bob doesn't see living in a smaller centre such as Birch Hills as a major drawback. He feels the company has done quite well in the small-town environment, and the advantages more than offset any disadvantages.

"The biggest benefit is access to high-quality staff," he reflects. "We have found that rural Saskatchewan has a lot of employable people who have a good work ethic and experience in the needle industry. They are creative, loyal, and hard working." Labour costs are the biggest cost to manufacturing, both in terms of wages and of lost production when the labour force is disgruntled or goes on strike. Compared to manufacturers in larger centres, Rugged Country has no labour problems at all, "which is a big plus and gives us a significant competitive advantage."

In 1997, the Cockwills completed a 3,200-square-foot expansion to their manufacturing location, providing space for increased production and a new embroidery machine. The company remains poised for significant growth, and is pursuing a range of interesting and unusual markets, including "turkey saddles" to protect hens during the mating season, and document pouches for funeral homes to provide to bereaved families.

Part of the expansion was necessary to house a new company, Country Leathers, that was officially launched in the spring of 1999. "This new venture began in August 1998 when we purchased Northwest Manufacturing and Glove of Paradise Hill, Saskatchewan," says Bob. The company had been producing gloves used by SaskPower and SaskTel, and Bob saw it as "an opportunity to bring in a complementary apparel and textile product line that would build on what we were already doing. At the time we thought hard about how we would manage this new company. Although we could see the marketing opportunities, we did not know anything about leather manufacturing."

As a result, the Cockwills brought Phil Marzo into the Country Leather venture. Phil, originally from Ontario, brought thirty years' experience in the glove business to the new venture. "Phil joined us as an equity partner and shareholder in Country Leather," says Bob. "This was absolutely the right thing for us to do. Phil has done a marvelous job with development of new leather products for a range of specialized markets." When they thought about it, they realized that a major part of their success with Rugged Country had been due to their staff, particularly Janet Van Zandbergen, who has been responsible for the design work and for managing all the sewing.

Country Leather is producing a range of gloves from several materials, including cowhide for work gloves and deerskin for fine dress gloves. They also produce custom-made and specialty orders for people who have fingers missing or hard-to-fit hands. One of the new products being developed is a bull-riding glove, which will no doubt be welcomed in rodeo circles. Wedding gloves and high-voltage gloves are already in stock.

Aside from excellence and expertise in their staff, the Cockwills feel that a key element to business success is future planning. "But to do that well," Bob warns, "you must thoroughly understand the industry you're working in." While he admits the apparel and textile industry has placed him on an extremely steep learning curve, he has made the time to take in as much as he can. He has, for example, been active in the Apparel & Textile Association of Saskatchewan (ATAS) and is currently vice president of the Board of Directors.

"Saskatchewan is a small place," he notes. "As a business person, you must become directly involved with the larger industry sector. It's a great way to meet other stakeholders in the industry, make a contribution to policy, and, most important, gain information about the sector.

"In today's economy," he reminds us, "information and knowledge translate directly into dollars."

Bob has taken his knowledge and new marketing technologies to heart. One of his next steps is to develop an Internet site to spread the word about Rugged Country and Country Leather, and possibly sell products online.

In January 2000, Country Embossing Ltd. opened with a state-of-the-art embossing machine for clothing and leathers. The only machine of its kind in western Canada, the German-made equipment is also capable of two-colour silk screens and flocking—"whatever the customer wants." In April 2000 Bob opened a new store in Prince Albert to expose their products and bring in new customers.

"But everything takes time," he advises, echoing successful entrepreneurs from everywhere. "You have to be patient, work hard, and make sure you have a good product and good people."

Then everything else should fall into place.

18

Earl Beebe Trucking Ltd.

I don't know how we managed. We were living on a farm thirteen kilometers outside Big River, had three small children and a rapidly growing trucking company, when my husband Earl died. We had just built a new company office, purchased several new trucks, and were carrying a huge debt.

— **Shirley Beebe**

SHIRLEY BEEBE and her husband Earl had started a trucking company to serve northern businesses. They started small and were in a major expansion mode when suddenly, in May 1985, Earl died. Shirley decided to carry on the business with the help from her sister, Deedie Lomsnes. The first thing she did was rent out the farm home, move into Big River, and reduce the debt load as much as possible. The company had developed a good relationship with some of the northern firms, and they committed themselves to stay with Shirley during the transition period.

"I suppose most people would have given up," Shirley reflects, "but it was part of a dream that Earl and I developed together. I knew we could do it."

Today, the company client list includes Weyerhaeuser Lumber, the Northwest Company, and the Freshwater Fish Marketing Board in Winnipeg. They haul up to four million pounds of fish per year in containers. They have a fleet of twelve heavy-duty trucks, two company owned and ten leased by the operators. They pull fourteen reefer vans, two log trailers, and one lowbed all over northern Saskatchewan. Keeping up the family tradition, her two sons and one daughter all play a role in the business.

"Earl and I were high school sweethearts," Shirley confides. "We married just out of high school. I took a year of university training with the goal of becoming a school teacher. Earl worked with a construction company hauling gravel. He soon decided that he didn't want to work for someone else. We had lots of ambition and energy and nothing to lose, so we started our own business."

They proved to be a dynamite team. "Earl had the smarts in operations," Shirley remembers, "and I had the smarts in business." In 1969, they established Earl Beebe Trucking Ltd. as 50-50 partners. They began with a logging operation in winter and hauling fresh fish from northern communities to Prince Albert in the summer. In 1972 they purchased a farm and started raising cattle year round, trucking only in the summer. The company experienced continual growth, and trucks were added to the fleet. Expansions were financed from farm equity and bank loans.

In 1976 they incorporated, with the ownership structure remaining the same. In 1978, Earl Beebe Trucking built a maintenance shop and car wash, which was financed through the Federal Business Development Bank. In 1979 they purchased a general freight hauling company from Big River, which expanded the fleet to ten trucks. Contracts were secured to haul freight from Saskatoon and Prince Albert to the northern communities of La Loche, Buffalo Narrows, Ile-à-la Crosse, and Pine House. The addition of back-haul runs, in which freight is trucked both to and from major centres, secured the place of Earl Beebe Trucking Ltd. as a major company in Big River. In 1983, Earl Beebe Trucking Ltd. expanded again, building a warehouse and office building in Big River.

Then, in 1985, Earl passed away, leaving Shirley, at the age of thirty-four, the sole owner of Earl Beebe Trucking Ltd. With children aged eight, ten, and twelve, she had a decision to make about the future of the company.

"There were so many factors to consider," she remembers. "I considered selling the business, but felt that, financially, the company was not in a good position, with the debt load it was carrying. I was concerned about what would happen to the employees."

Earl and Shirley had dreamed of seeing their family raised in the business. From Shirley's perspective, as both a mother and a sudden widow, changing careers could not provide the same flexibility that she had with Earl Beebe Trucking. "I had always been in charge, and didn't believe I could adapt well to working for someone else. Living in Big River with my family was important to me, and I needed to be in control. After examining all my options, I decided to keep Earl Beebe Trucking Ltd. and to operate it myself."

She could not, however, manage her young family, run the business, and continue to live on their farm, so she built a house in town near the office and

One of a fleet of twelve heavy-duty trucks that are operated by Earl Beebe Trucking Ltd., based in Big River, SK.

rented out the farm. She continues to own the farm, so the children will have an opportunity to live on it in the future if they choose.

That decision made, Shirley had to determine how to operate the business and still manage her other responsibilities. According to Shirley, Earl had been committed to the business and spent a great deal of time making sure it would be successful. But he didn't know how to delegate. He wanted to control the operations. Shirley had always been more community and family-oriented. She knew she had to run the company differently than Earl had.

"When you're married to your job, you forget about living and don't really experience life," says Shirley. "My family needed parental support. My oldest son is handicapped, and, at that time, required additional time and attention. My children had just lost their father, and I was determined that they would not lose their mother, too."

Shirley learned to delegate responsibility to employees, putting them in charge of certain areas of the operation, especially driving and maintenance, where she lacked the skill and knowledge that Earl had brought to the job. That left her time both to be with her family and to do the things she was good at. For marketing, for example, Earl Beebe Trucking relies on its reputation and excellent service. When problems arise, Shirley likes to deal with them as soon as they happen. "I do what I can to make the customer happy," she says. "Since it is a small business, it is easier to get a hold of me than if you were dealing with a big corporation." With a staff of twenty, including drivers, three mechanics, and four office staff, Shirley does not find a large amount of conflict. If there are problems, she likes to analyze them, look at all aspects, and then find the appropriate solution for everyone.

Shirley does not take big risks. "I have to take care of my employees. They expect to get paid, and if I take risks, I jeopardize my company and the security of my staff."

The company's main source of capital is the money that comes in from trucking. When purchasing new equipment, they make sure they can afford it. When making financial and managerial decisions, Shirley relies on her thirty years of experience. She finds that she is something of a conservative manager. She would rather spend money in improving the equipment than worry about expanding. Expansions take too long to pay off, she feels, and she would rather expand the business as she can afford to.

When Earl and Shirley started their business, they had great feedback from their community, so they were able to put together a good work force and create jobs. They had no real competition. There were—and are—other trucking companies, but they specialized in different areas.

Earl Beebe Trucking operates within clearly defined parameters that meet the needs and objectives of the owner, the employees, and the community. Their market niche is to serve the freight-hauling needs of small northern communities. "We have carefully identified the needs of our customers and targeted our services," Shirley explains. The company will continue to be based in Big River in order to maintain direct links with the northern communities and guarantee the quality and flexibility that the customers have come to expect.

Shirley's future plans are to be able to keep twenty employees and, if the opportunity arises, perhaps get bigger...gradually. She sees service, hands-on management, and good employees as the keys to her success, as well as keeping the equipment maintained and the organization running smoothly. She has established a good name in a business she is proud of. She hopes someday her children will take it over, and possibly expand.

"Controlled growth fits my philosophy of balancing all aspects of life," says Shirley. "Too many business owners work eighteen-hour days simply to pay the bills. It's important for business owners and employees to enjoy life and not be consumed by work. It's important to maintain health and happiness, as we only have one chance at life."

The difficulties she faces are related to location, large competitors, and politics. As in all businesses, there are advantages and disadvantages to being in a certain location. An advantage for locating the company in Saskatchewan is that she is from Saskatchewan and this is where she wants to live. A disadvantage is that Saskatchewan is a highly taxed province, a fact that scares other entrepreneurs away. "It might be better to be in a bigger place," Shirley philosophizes, "but then you will have more problems as well." You have to make your own way, she feels: "Everyone has problems. It's how you handle those problems that can give you an advantage, regardless of the location."

Shirley was one of two finalists for the 1996 Canadian Women Entrepreneurs of the Year Awards. To young entrepreneurs, she says that having your own business is challenging but rewarding. "Think about your goals and how you want to achieve them. Don't worry about the roadblocks. Problems give you experience."

She is herself the proof of her philosophy. Faced with sudden tragedy and irrecoverable loss, she quickly put together a competent management team of people she trusted.

"Shirley's common-sense and straightforward approach to doing business are appreciated by all who work with her," according to her banker, Mr. Senger of the Hong Kong Bank of Canada. "She is admired and respected for managing a successful business in a male-dominated industry. Further accolades are due her when you consider that she has balanced the operation of the business with raising her family."

According to Shirley, gender is not as much of an issue as it used to be. Fifteen years ago she was unique in the business community; today there are many women in senior positions, and Shirley finds herself negotiating contracts with women as often as she does with men. There are fewer barriers to women today, and the opportunities are tremendous throughout Saskatchewan.

Shirley is proud of her three children, now adults, who are very involved in the business. Each of them, at one time or another, has gone away to school or to work, but they have all come back to the family business. Shirley hopes to turn things over to them within the next ten years.

☾

Afterword

"Life is not about success and rewards, but it is about dealing with fear, moving through personal and public failure, helping others, and living with passion."

Anonymous

IF I have learned one thing from researching this book, it is that entrepreneurs are not afraid to try new things. In practical terms, this means they are also not afraid of failure. Like Thomas Edison, Henry Ford, and other successful innovators, they think of their "mistakes" or "failures" as simply discovering one more way that something will not work and then continue to look for new approaches to the problem or to building their business.

There is no secret to running and operating a successful business or enterprise. The factors critical to starting one are repeatedly outlined in textbooks, popular business books, and all the business and entrepreneurial magazines. We have all read them from time to time, but I believe most people do not understand how to apply these crucial elements to their own situation.

The current trends in the global economy are rapidly changing from fewer "employment" opportunities to more "self-employment" opportunities. Working people of all ages must prepare for a time when self-employment will be the best option for financial security. Many of us, young and old, will be required to run our own business. How can we best prepare? One way is to learn from those around us who already have the knowledge and skill sets to start new business ventures.

What I have learned from writing this book is that the primary qualities contributing to success are "in the mind" and include such psychological attributes as passion, vision, drive, persistence, tenacity, motivation, self-confidence, a positive attitude, and personal initiative. The entrepreneurs in this book are successful because they embody some of the psychological attributes needed to succeed. Their drive and focus, based on a powerful "can do" attitude, provide the foundation for achievement. Henry Ford's famous observation often came to mind as I the interviewed the entrepreneurs in this book: "If you think you can, or think you can't, you're right!" This idea underscores the necessity for a strong personal belief and a positive approach to problem solving.

The secondary factors contributing to forming and running successful businesses are more concrete and can be termed "activities." These activities include market assessment, feasibility studies, business plans, and planning related to consideration of managerial features and functions. These secondary factors are sometimes rated as highly as the psychological attributes listed above, but in the case of some of the enterprises in this book, had they placed the secondary factors too high, the businesses would never have begun. Most of the ideas in this book were new and innovative, and the marketplace research likely indicated "it isn't needed" or "it can't be done." Don't get me wrong. Market research and business planning are important, but they are secondary features and do not alone lead to a successful enterprise.

In a nutshell, these entrepreneurs are successful for three reasons: they wanted to be successful, they believed they would be successful, and they did whatever it took to achieve their goals of success.

Although there are many entrepreneurial successes across rural Saskatchewan, we tried to take into account geography, culture, gender, and various economic sectors in order to feature a range of critical factors needed to succeed. Here are the highlights and the main points from each of the chapters.

Community Ventures

1. Quadra Group

- *Think Big*: At the beginning, the Quadra partners decided to be a major player in the pork sector for western Canada, basing development and expansion on global trends for meat production and consumption. They saw the potential for enormous growth.

This vision was the starting point, which provided the framework for the planning that followed.

- *Change Management*: The Quadra partners had ideas about what they wanted to do but not necessarily how to do it. Richard Wright talks about the concept of "Ready, Fire, Aim." The point is that you must prepare well and then go forward with the understanding that you must make directional changes and adjustments as you go.

- *Leadership*: Wright also points out that not everyone has to be a leader or a community champion. "We only need 10% of the population to be strong leaders, but the other 90% must be prepared to support leaders in order to build successful enterprises and communities." He uses the analogy of the body. The head or brain may provide the thinking and direction, but every other part of the body must do their part perfectly and in harmony in order to perform with peak effectiveness and efficiency.

2. Manitou Springs Hotel & Mineral Spa

- *Risk Taking*: Benjamin Disraeli once said, "Don't be afraid to leap when required. You cannot cross a chasm in two steps." The steering committee that rebuilt Manitou Springs Hotel & Mineral Spa after the fire might well have used this as a motto. They had the personal confidence to move forward at great personal risk on behalf of the community: they commenced the planning studies and building before they had all the resources in place. It worked.

- *Bold Action*: In order to create some momentum for action, a patient and cautious approach to rebuilding Manitou Springs Hotel & Mineral Spa would not have worked, and the committee was not afraid to act boldly. They failed a number of times but never gave up. They learned from what did not work and continually sought new approaches. Because the committee was willing to move boldly with confidence and enthusiasm, their action, based on a strong belief in success, became a self-fulfilling prophecy.

3. Meadow Lake Tribal Council

- *Belief in First Nations*: The future success of Saskatchewan will be based on learning how to work with First Nations people. As a province, we are already short of skilled labour in most sectors and our opportunity for economic growth is within the large, emerging First Nations work force. There are great challenges but also great opportunities for those who believe in the future of all Saskatchewan people working together.

- *Community Leadership*: Bold and courageous leadership by both community and business was the key factor in the success of the NorSask sawmill. This direction from the aboriginal and non-aboriginal communities was respected and had integrity. The leaders developed a vision they were able to effectively communicate and share with the community. The communities were looking for direction and responded with loyal support when it was provided.

4. Big Quill Resources Inc.

- *Power of a Dream*: Success is not always financial. It is also proving that a community can make its own way. They can take steps to change, independent of government policies and decisions. The belief that a community can influence its own development is the foundation for trying innovative ventures built in new creative ways. Some of these ventures may not succeed, but dreams are the basis for planning and action. As the motivational speaker Robert Schuller summarizes it, "If you can first 'conceive' and 'believe' you will 'achieve'!"

- *Community Resources*: Part of instituting the dream for Big Quill was the recognition that the Wynyard community already had all the human resources required to research, plan, design, build, and operate an innovative, state-of-the-art, manufacturing plant. Based on a strong belief in the innovative capabilities of local people and supported by the right training and encouragement, the belief in the dream was fulfilled.

5. West Central Pelleting Ltd.

- *Community Alliances*: Forget the past hockey wars and community rivalry. Individual communities are on a downward spiral because, by themselves, they are often too small to support large business ventures. The mutual collaboration of the towns of Wilkie and Unity, and the surrounding rural municipalities (RMs) resulted in the development of five major business enterprises. The impact of a handful of strong community leaders with a vision of what could be, supported by the majority of the community, made all the difference.

- *Never Give Up*: There were enormous challenges in establishing a working relationship between the communities of Wilkie and Unity, and the surrounding RMs, despite the many good reasons to do so. One reason the leaders in both communities prevailed was because they had a definition of community that was more regional than local. Although this point of view was difficult to implement, they did not give up. One key strategy that supported development in both communities was to offer low-value shares, which meant local people in each community became shareholders and consequently cheerleaders for the community projects.

6. Kitsaki Management Limited Partnership

- *Profits First*: "Profits must be foremost on our minds, in regard to economic development. I have never considered economic development opportunities unless profits were considered first, because without profits, you cannot expand and you cannot create employment." Chief Harry Cook, Lac La Ronge Indian Band.

- *Partnership and Alliances*: Chief Cook believes that through partnership or alliances missing areas of expertise can be filled in: "Everyone has strengths and abilities to bring to the table. You may be missing many of the skill sets, but they can be acquired through creative partnerships, alliances, and other innovative arrangements. Use your imagination. Anything is possible if there is a vision and the drive to succeed."

Group Ventures

7. Lakeside Machinery Co-operative Ltd.

- *Farming for Profit:* A machinery co-op was a creative solution to the farm financial crisis in the early 1970s. This co-op succeeded where many others failed for a number of reasons. There was open communication among all partners, which was the basis for good relations among them. There was also a sharing of resources and expertise. A key factor in the success of the co-op was the use of professionals (accountants and lawyers) in the start-up of the venture. The structure developed by these professionals allowed partners to join and leave the co-op. In addition, a mechanism was developed that allowed partners to retire with equity. Another important feature of the structure allowed young people join the co-op without equity.

- *Corporate Alliances*: Glen Laxdal advises: "Do not be afraid to negotiate a business or market alliance with a major player in the agribusiness sector." There can be "win-wins" in a broad range of areas that can form the basis for a good working relationship. The relationships can be short term or long term. As a small group of farmers, Lakeside brought valuable partnership strengths to the negotiating table that were recognized and appreciated by large agribusiness companies.

8. Delsa Food Processors Inc.

- *Creating Your Own Future*: Delsa Food Processors Inc. grew out of an understanding of the impending changes in global agriculture and the declining profitability in a commodity-based agricultural system. The partners knew that some type of value-added product was essential for long-term survival in Saskatchewan agriculture. They also knew they must take initiative rather than wait for government direction or assistance.

- *Try and Try Again*: Originally, the group had an idea for mustard processing that ultimately was not feasible. In attempting to develop the mustard-processing venture, they stumbled on vegetable processing using products locally produced. They made a number of mistakes along the way, but learned a great deal and maximized the resources offered by a Dutch partner. They continue to learn and take new approaches to a dynamic and growing market.

9. Rose Bush Acres

- *Adjusting to Change*: Business enterprises come and go but the entrepreneurs behind the venture survive and go on to other things. Rose Bush Acres was the fulfillment of a particular dream for four entrepreneurs. Although profitable, operating the business using employees was difficult. Recently the business was sold to a couple who operate the bed and breakfast as owner-managers, which was part of the original vision and a more cost-effective way to run the venture.

- *A Strong "Why"*: It was clear to the proponents of Rose Bush Acres that they wanted a destination tourist venture but they were not sure how it would unfold. When the time came, they had the ability to make very quick decisions. Entrepreneurship may appear illogical at times, but the primary factors so important in the make-up of true entrepreneurs now become all important. In the case of this group they kept going when it looked hopeless and they made it happen through will.

- *Creative Financing*: You must be prepared to finance your business venture and take creative steps to obtain other equity or financing if required. Rose Bush Acres established a unique heritage co-op to utilize community resources through sweat equity and raise the additional capital for the required renovations and professional services.

10. Pound-Maker Agventures Ltd.

- *Self-Reliance*: Initiated during the farm crisis of the early 1970s, the community leaders who developed Pound-Maker Agventures Ltd. were determined to find diversified and value-added ventures to reduce the reliance on commodities and the export market. Although they faced adversity and setbacks, they took responsibility for their situation and created their future. They were not afraid to think big and do things that had not been done before.

- *Market Access Through Alliances*: The proponents were farmers with limited expertise in large business but with a vision for a diversified local market. They recognized the benefits of strategic alliances with corporate partners who could provide the needed technology, investment capital, and access to markets. They found that a small group of farmers working as a team could be a strong partner in negotiating with large multinational companies.

11. Sandhills Essence

- *Partnerships and Communication*: The partners had major disadvantages to overcome: they lived some distance from each other and were developing a rural-based business in a unique and newly emerging market. They developed their products and marketing strategy to suit the growth and needs of the company. The primary factor in their success was the very different but complementary skill sets each partner brought to the business. This factor was multiplied by a strong and open communication policy that focused on internal dispute resolution and business problem solving.

- *Creative Focus and Personal Initiative*: Despite a remote rural location, the three partners established and expanded a successful business, based on a need for an alternate income. They developed their enterprise in a manner that accommodated young families and their family farm business, and was based on continuous product development and improvement. They did this with no debt, carefully expanding as they generated profits and retained earnings. This was done with focus, commitment to the business and to each other, common goals, and personal initiative.

Individual Ventures

12. Husband's Foods

- *Enjoy What You Do*: Carol Husband says there are farm business opportunities everywhere. Look at your personal skill sets, your interests, your support network, and pick a business you enjoy. Believe in what you do. Go at it with passion and enthusiasm, which is contagious and will be passed on to your customers. Don't be afraid of what the neighbours will think.

- *Know Your Customer*: A major key to the Husbands' success was getting to know all their customers on a personal basis. This is a very different approach from that taken by most farmers who know very little about the end users of their products. The Husbands' experience in personal selling started with their purebred beef business when they learned additional margins could be achieved when selling directly to domestic and international buyers. They have successfully expanded this marketing approach with their organic farming business.

- *Willingness to Change*: When the Husbands looked for an alternate farm enterprise to the cattle business, they researched the choices and selected organic farming, primarily for business reasons. They knew they could make a good living in this sector, but it meant running their farm and marketing their products in a very different manner. Carol warns that adaptation takes time and costs money. Anyone in business must anticipate ongoing changes in their industry, and although the best time to consider change is before your back is against the wall, there are always options if you are willing to change.

13. Last Mountain Berry Farms Inc.

- *Saskatchewan's Business Advantage*: Barry Isaac believes that no matter where you do business, there are advantages and disadvantages. However, he believes the Saskatchewan business advantages clearly outweigh the disadvantages and this is a key factor in the success of their business in a rural location. He says, "You often hear complaints about taxes and regulations, but there are many other tangible benefits that work to our advantage such as a great work force and a central location in a rapidly growing western Canadian market."

- *Focus on Quality*: A major factor in the growth of the Last Mountain Berry Farms is the "home grown" quality and taste derived from traditional processing with no artificial preservatives. Barry says, "We invested a great deal of effort in producing a quality product and the results are there."

- *Market Alliances*: Because the Issacs had a good understanding of the food marketing system and were able to take advantage of marketing programs for "Saskatchewan Made" and "Canadian Made" products, they have successfully marketed their products. Ascertaining consumer preferences and market trends with food retailers and negotiating win-win relations was key to market success. "Don't be afraid to talk to the big players in any industry," says Barry, "they often need an alliance with a small niche player."

14. Drake Meat Processors Inc.

- *Product Innovation*: Many people comment that the Saskatchewan population base is too small to sustain a domestic market. Drake Meat has proven that a company can be successful and grow inside the provincial market. The factors contributing to their success are a good understanding the market, finding their niche, and focusing on continued research and development, and innovative market alliances.

- *Make Mistakes Sooner*: President Kelly Ediger recommends new entrepreneurs prepare to make mistakes and make them earlier. He believes the fastest way to grow and to learn is to "try, try, and try some more." Kelly says you have to understand that sometimes things do not work out the first or second or third time. Echoing the American humourist Mark Twain, Kelly says that if he had a chance to do the business over, he would make many of the same mistakes but he would make them sooner.

15. Riese's Canadian Lake Wild Rice

- *Think Big*: Lynn Riese observes, "We became the largest Canadian lake wild rice exporters because that was our goal. You only become the best or the most creative or the most innovative by establishing that as your goal and target. Aim high! The marketplace can be cruel but there are also a great many opportunities if you take the initiative to meet your customers, find out what they want and deliver quality. Your customers can be your best friends and will refer other business."

- *Sense of Humour*: Lynn believes that any new business will face obstacles (which may appear insurmountable), and he knows that along the way entrepreneurs face many reasons to quit. However, he also believes that entrepreneurs are innovators and problem solvers: "Sometimes the answer is direct action and other times it takes patience to wait for a problem to work itself out. Be creative, have fun and maintain a healthy sense of humour."

- *Self-Confidence*: Finally, Lynn advises, "Try and try again. Persistence was the key element of our success. I wanted to develop a business in La Ronge, where I was born and raised, and make a contribution to the community. We are not the best location to run an international export business but I was determined to make it work. It takes strong self-confidence and a belief in yourself and your abilities." Here again, we see the importance of the primary factors for success: tenacity, self-confidence, positive attitude, motivation.

16. Banach Winery

- *Persistence*: Although the Banachs did not clearly understand what they were getting into by turning a hobby into a business, they, too, had some of the important primary factors for success—persistence, tenacity. They also exhibit some of the secondary factors that were a help to them: they had the technology to produce their wine and understood the importance of setting a high standard in the quality of their product. They also had a sense that there was an emerging niche market for their wines as well as a market among tourists. They succeeded because they were persistent and did not give up.

- *Creativity*: Their advice is, "Don't let obstacles get you down. If you stay positive and optimistic, your mind will be open to creative solutions, which are key to success. We started a business that did not exist before. We ran into the 'it can't be done' comment a number of times. We had to overcome many obstacles such as changing the provincial legislation. It is amazing what can be done with an open mind and a creative approach."

17. Rugged Country Manufacturing

- *Acquire Expertise*: The Cockwills worked "incredibly hard" the first years and developed their initial product line through trial and error. A key factor to their success was that at the outset they hired skilled seamstresses and natural innovators who were often better problem solvers than the Cockwills themselves. Together, the skilled staff and the Cockwills looked for ways to do everything better through innovation and creativity.

- *Partners and Niche Market Alliances*: The leather business developed because of a series of opportunities. One reason for success was that the Cockwills entered a business partnership with Phil Marzo who had expertise in the leather glove business. Bob Cockwill believes that without Phil they could never have succeeded in the glove business. He notes, "Our partner helped negotiate long-term contracts with specific users of special order leather gloves and led continuous product development and improvement."

18. Earl Beebe Trucking Ltd.

- *Focus*: Shirley had to make some quick decisions following her husband's death. She decided to rent the farm and focus all her energies on her young family first and the trucking business second. She had the advantage of an understanding of the financial side of the business and was determined to make it work. The key to success was her vision for the business and her single-minded focus on the tasks at hand.

- *Delegation and Networking*: Due to her family commitments, Shirley could not work full time at the business. She surrounded herself with people she trusted and who had complementary skill sets. By delegating key responsibilities to these like-minded people she was able to build the business around her vision. She communicated her vision with suppliers and customers to develop a network of mutual support for her business.

- *Quality of Life:* "You must have balance in your life. Despite the challenges and rigours of business, do not forget quality time for your family and for yourself. As an entrepreneur you will be a much more creative and effective business leader if you have a balanced personal life. In the larger picture, success in life is much more important than success in business. My business success may not last but my success as a 'person of quality' will, and must, last."

Summary

It was a pleasure to get to know a few of Saskatchewan's solid core of entrepreneurs who are making a difference. It is a relief to know that a strong entrepreneurial attitude is scattered in every corner of the province, made up of people who are doing what many would say, "is not needed" or "can't be done." I hope this book plays a small role in launching a flurry of business start-ups in all sectors, by people of all ages and backgrounds, in all parts of the province.

"Will the last person to leave please turn out the lights!" has often been heard uttered in only a semi-jocular way by those who doubt our capabilities and the potential economy and marketplace in Saskatchewan. Today, Saskatchewan entrepreneurs are on the move with a vision and commitment to building a bright future for themselves, their community and the province. The entrepreneurs in this book have shown that, while it may mean solving some problems by locating a business in a rural area, with creativity, persistence, faith, and a good understanding of the marketplace, it is possible to succeed in your own backyard. There is lots of room for new businesses in our great province. Why not consider following your dreams and join these innovative modern pioneers?

Appendix:
Key Contacts and Addresses

Community Ventures

1. **Quadra Group, Outlook**
   Richard Wright, President
   Quadra Group
   P.O. Box 638, 500 Progress Avenue
   Outlook, SK S0L 2N0
   Tel: (306) 867•8916
   Fax: (306) 867•8917
   E-mail: rwright@quadragroup.sk.ca

2. **Manitou Springs Hotel & Mineral Spa, Manitou Beach/Watrous**
   Dale Hayter, Owner
   Manitou Springs Hotel and Mineral Spa
   P.O. Box 610
   Watrous, SK S0K 4T0
   Tel: (306) 946•2233
   Fax: (306) 946•2554
   E-mail: manitousprings@sk.sympatico.ca
   www.manitouspringsspa.sk.ca

3. **Meadow Lake Tribal Council, Meadow Lake**
   Vern Bachiu, Director, Policy & Development
   Meadow Lake Tribal Council
   8003 Flying Dust First Nation
   Meadow Lake, SK S9X 1T8
   Tel: (306) 236•5654
   Fax: (306) 236•6301
   E-mail: vern.bachiu@mltc.net
   www. mltc.net

4. **Big Quill Resources Inc., Wynyard**
   Harvey Haugen, President
   Big Quill Resources Inc.
   P.O. Box 1059
   Wynyard, SK S0A 4T0
   Tel: (306) 554•3322
   Fax: (306) 554•3858
   E-mail: harvey@bigquill.com
   www.bigquill.com

5. **West Central Pelleting Ltd., Wilkie**
   Margaret Skinner, President
   West Central Pelleting Ltd.
   P.O. Box 671
   Wilkie, SK S0K 4W0
   Tel: (306) 843•3490
   Fax: (306) 843•2810
   E-mail: wcp@sk.sympatico.ca

6. **Kitsaki Management Limited Partnership, La Ronge**
Al Solheim, Director of Finance
Kitsaki Management Limited Partnership
P.O. Box 480
La Ronge, SK S0J 1L0
Tel: (306) 425•2183 Saskatoon Tel: (306) 477•4599
Fax: (306) 425•2590 Saskatoon Fax: (306) 242•6988
E-mail: kitsaki@dlcwest.com
www.kitsaki.com

Group Ventures

7. **Lakeside Machinery Co-operative Ltd., Dafoe**
Glen Laxdal, Director, Market Development
Lakeside Machinery Co-operative Ltd.
P.O. Box 1660
Wynyard, SK S0A 4T0
Tel: (306) 554•2078
Fax: (306) 554•2867
E-mail: lakeside@sk.sympatico.ca
http://@agripulse.com/
www.lakesidespecialcrops.com

8. **Delsa Food Processors Inc., Delisle**
Syd Hill, President
Delsa Food Processors Inc.
P.O. Box 489
Delisle, SK S0L 0P0
Tel: (306) 493•2400
Fax: (306) 493•2211
E-mail: delsa@delsa.sk.ca

9. Rose Bush Acres, Watson

Earl & Perla Werk, Owners
Rose Bush Acres
P.O. Box 327
Watson, SK S0K 4V0
Tel: (306) 287•3362
Fax: (306) 287•4221
E-mail: stay@rosebushacres.8m.com

10. Pound-Maker Agventures Ltd., Lanigan

Mylles Wildeman, Chair, Board of Directors
Pound-Maker Agventures Ltd.
P.O. Box 519
Lanigan, SK S0K 2M0
Tel: (306) 365•4281 Res. Tel: (306) 365•4695
Fax: (306) 365•4283 Res. Fax: (306) 365•4697
E-mail: m.t.wildeman@sk.sympatico.ca

11. Sandhills Essence, Hazlet

Janice Stock, Partner
Sandhills Essence
P.O. Box 32
Hazlet, SK S0N 1E0
Tel: (306) 678•4810
Fax: (306) 678•4810
E-mail: see website
www.sandhillsessence.sk.ca

Individual Ventures

12. Husband's Foods, Wawota

Carol Husband, Co-owner
Husband's Foods
P.O. Box 32
Wawota, SK S0G 5A0
Tel: (306) 739 • 2900
Fax: (306) 739 • 2900
E-mail: husbandsfoods@sk.sympatico.ca

13. Last Mountain Berry Farms Inc., Southey

Barbara Isaac, President
Last Mountain Berry Farms Inc.
RR #1, Box 12
Southey, SK S0G 4P0
Tel: (306) 726 • 4683
Fax: (306) 726 • 4678
E-mail: berry.farms@sk.sympatico.ca
www.lastmountainberryfarms.com

14. Drake Meat Processors Inc., Drake

Kelley Ediger, President
Drake Meat Processors Ltd.
P.O. Box 29
Drake, SK S0K 1H0
Tel: (306) 363 • 2117
Fax: (306) 363 • 2119
E-mail: drake.meats@sk.sympatico.ca

15. **Riese's Canadian Lake Wild Rice, La Ronge**
K. Lynn Riese, President
Riese's Canadian Lake Wild Rice
P.O. Box 899
La Ronge, SK S0J 1L0
Tel: (306) 425•2314
Fax: (306) 425•2061
E-mail: riese@sk.sympatico.ca
www.northweb.sk.ca/riese

16. **Banach Winery, Battleford**
Walter & Diane Banach, Co-owners
Banach Winery
P.O. Box 1853, 22nd Street West
Battleford, SK S0M 0E0
Tel: (306) 445•9463
Fax: (306) 445•7782

17. **Rugged Country Manufacturing, Birch Hills**
Bob Cockwill, President
Rugged Country Manufacturing
P.O. Box 809
Birch Hills, SK S0J 0G0
Tel: (306) 749•3511
Fax: (306) 749•3544
E-mail: rugged@sk.sympatico.ca

18. **Earl Beebe Trucking Ltd., Big River**
Shirley Beebe, President
Earl Beebe Trucking Ltd.
P.O. Box 429
Big River, SK S0J 0E0
Tel: (306) 469•2289
Fax: (306) 469•4848